MW01671934

Artists of the Futurist Movement: Goncharova, Malevich, Boccioni, Dottori, et. al.

Jenny Reese

The role of the book within our culture is changing. The change is brought on by new ways to acquire & use content, the rapid dissemination of information and real-time peer collaboration on a global scale. Despite these changes one thing is clear--"the book" in it's traditional form continues to play an important role in learning and communication. The book you are holding in your hands utilizes the unique characteristics of the Internet -- relying on web infrastructure and collaborative tools to share and use resources in keeping with the characteristics of the medium (user-created, defying control, etc.)--while maintaining all the convenience and utility of a real book.

Contents

Articles

References

Futurism

Futurism

Futurism was an artistic and social movement that originated in Italy in the early 20th century. It was largely an Italian phenomenon, though there were parallel movements in Russia, England and elsewhere. The Futurists practiced in every medium of art, including painting, sculpture, ceramics, graphic design, industrial design, interior design, theatre, film, fashion, textiles, literature, music, architecture and even gastronomy.

Futurism in Italy 1909-1916

The founder of Futurism and its most influential personality was the Italian writer Filippo Tommaso Marinetti. Marinetti launched the movement in his *Futurist Manifesto*, which he published for the first time on 5 February 1909 in *La gazzetta dell'Emilia*, an article then reproduced in the French daily newspaper *Le Figaro* on 20 February 1909. He was soon joined by the painters Umberto Boccioni, Carlo Carrà, Giacomo Balla, Gino Severini and the composer Luigi Russolo.

Marinetti expressed a passionate loathing of everything old, especially political and artistic tradition. "We want no part of it, the past", he wrote, "we the young and strong *Futurists!*" The Futurists admired speed, technology, youth and violence, the car, the airplane and the industrial city, all that represented the technological triumph of humanity over nature, and they were passionate nationalists. They repudiated the cult of the past and all imitation, praised originality, "however daring, however violent", bore proudly "the smear of madness", dismissed art critics as useless, rebelled against harmony and good taste, swept away all the themes and subjects of all previous art, and gloried in science.

Publishing manifestos was a feature of Futurism, and the Futurists (usually led or prompted by Marinetti) wrote them on many topics, including painting, architecture, religion, clothing and cooking.

The founding manifesto did not contain a positive artistic programme, which the Futurists attempted to create in their subsequent *Technical Manifesto of Futurist Painting*. This committed them to a "universal dynamism", which was to be directly represented in painting. Objects in reality were not separate from one another or from their surroundings: "The sixteen people around you in a rolling motor bus are in turn and at the same time one, ten four three; they are motionless and they change places. ... The motor bus rushes into the houses which it passes, and in their turn the houses throw themselves upon the motor bus and are blended with it."

The Futurist painters were slow to develop a distinctive style and subject matter. In 1910 and 1911 they used the techniques of Divisionism, breaking light and color down into a field of stippled dots and stripes, which had been originally created by Giovanni Segantini and others. Later, Severini, who lived in Paris, attributed their backwardness in style and method at this time to their distance from Paris, the centre of avant garde art. Severini was the first to come into contact with Cubism and following a visit to Paris in 1911 the Futurist painters adopted the methods of the Cubists. Cubism offered them a means of analysing energy in paintings and expressing dynamism.

They often painted modern urban scenes. Carrà's *Funeral of the Anarchist Galli* (1910-11) is a large canvas representing events that the artist had himself been involved in in 1904. The action of a police attack and riot is rendered energetically with diagonals and broken planes. His *Leaving the Theatre* (1910-11) uses a Divisionist technique to render isolated and faceless figures trudging home at night under street lights.

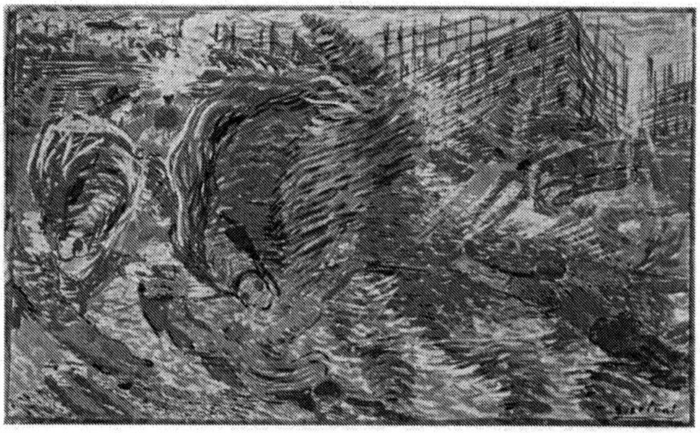

Umberto Boccioni, *The City Rises* (1910)

Boccioni's *The City Rises* (1910) represents scenes of construction and manual labour with a huge, rearing red horse in the centre foreground, which workmen struggle to control. His *States of Mind*, in three large panels, *The Farewell*, *Those who Go*, and *Those Who Stay*, "made his first great statement of Futurist painting, bringing his interests in Bergson, Cubism and the individual's complex experience of the modern world together in what has been described as one of the 'minor masterpieces' of early twentieth century painting." The work attempts to convey feelings and sensations experienced in time, using new means of expression, including "lines of force", which were intended to convey the directional tendencies of objects through space, "simultaneity", which combined memories, present impressions and anticipation of future events, and "emotional ambience" in which the artist seeks by intuition to link sympathies between the exterior scene and interior emotion.

Boccioni's intentions in art were strongly influenced by the ideas of Bergson, including the idea of intuition, which Bergson defined as a simple, indivisible experience of sympathy through which one is moved into the inner being of an object to grasp what is unique and ineffable within it. The Futurists aimed through their art thus to enable the viewer to apprehend the inner being of what they depicted. Boccioni developed these ideas at length in his book, *Pittura scultura Futuriste: Dinamismo plastico* (*Futurist Painting Sculpture: Plastic Dynamism*) (1914).

Balla's of a Dog on a Leash [1] (1912) exemplifies the Futurists' insistence that the perceived world is in constant movement. The painting depicts a dog whose legs, tail and leash - and the feet of the person walking it - have been multiplied to a blur of movement. It illustrates the precepts of the *Technical Manifesto of Futurist Painting* that, "On account of the persistency of an image upon the retina, moving objects constantly multiply themselves; their form changes like rapid vibrations, in their mad career. Thus a running horse has not four legs, but twenty, and their movements are triangular." His *Rhythm of the Bow* (1912) similarly depicts the movements of a violinist's hand and instrument, rendered in rapid strokes within a triangular frame.

The adoption of Cubism determined the style of much subsequent Futurist painting, which Boccioni and Severini in particular continued to render in the broken colors and short brush-strokes of divisionism. But Futurist painting differed in both subject matter and treatment from the quiet and static Cubism of Picasso, Braque and Gris. Although there were Futurist portraits (e.g. Carrà's *Woman with Absinthe* (1911), Severini's *Self-Portrait* (1912), and Boccioni's *Matter* (1912)), it was the urban scene and vehicles in motion that typified Futurist painting - e.g. Boccioni's *The Street Enters the House* (1911), Severini's *Dynamic Hieroglyph of the Bal Tabarin* (1912), and Russolo's *Automobile at Speed* (1913)

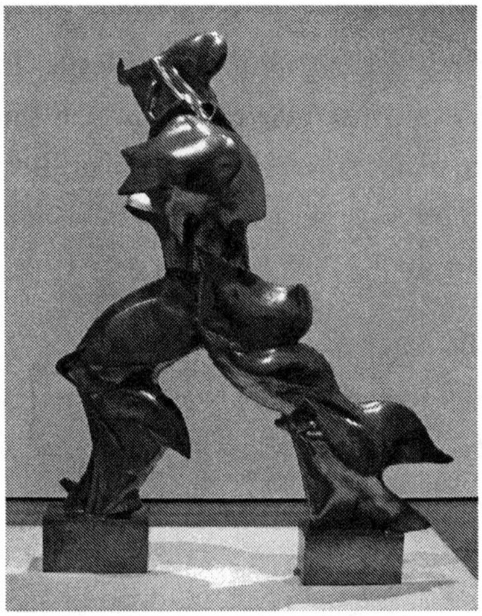

Umberto Boccioni, *Unique Forms of Continuity in Space* (1913)

In 1912 and 1913, Boccioni turned to sculpture to translate into three dimensions his Futurist ideas. In *Unique Forms of Continuity in Space* (1913) he attempted to realise the relationship between the object and its environment, which was central to his theory of "dynamism". The sculpture represents a striding figure, cast in bronze posthumously and exhibited in the Tate Gallery. (It now appears on the national side of Italian 20 eurocent coins). He explored the theme further in *Synthesis of Human Dynamism* (1912), *Speeding Muscles* (1913) and *Spiral Expansion of Speeding Muscles* (1913). His ideas on sculpture were published in the *Technical Manifesto of Futurist Sculpture* In 1915 Balla also turned to sculpture making abstract "reconstructions", which were created out of various materials, were apparently moveable and even made noises. He said that, after making twenty pictures in which he had studied the velocity of automobiles, he understood that "the single plane of the canvas did not permit the suggestion of the dynamic volume of speed in depth ... I felt the need to construct the first dynamic plastic complex with iron wires, cardboard planes, cloth and tissue paper, etc."

In 1914, personal quarrels and artistic differences between the Milan group, around Marinetti, Boccioni, and Balla, and the Florence group, around Carrà, Ardengo Soffici (1879-1964) and Giovanni Papini (1881-1956), created a rift in Italian Futurism. The Florence group resented the dominance of Marinetti and Boccioni, whom they accused of trying to establish "an immobile church with an infallible creed", and each group dismissed the other as *passéiste*.

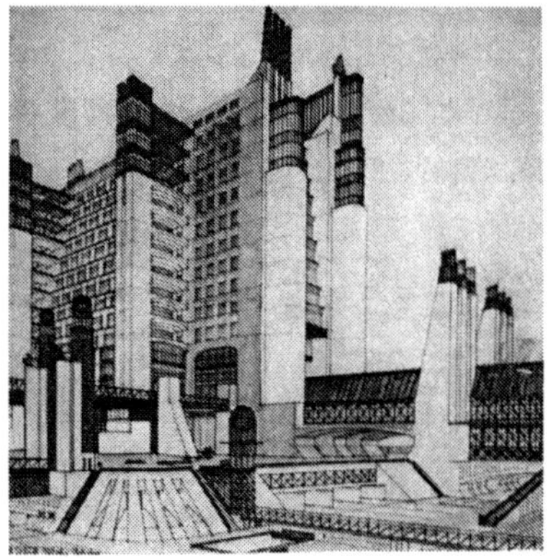

An example of Futurist architecture by Antonio Sant'Elia

Futurism had from the outset admired violence and was intensely patriotic. The *Futurist Manifesto* had declared, "We will glorify war - the world's only hygiene - militarism, patriotism, the destructive gesture of freedom-bringers, beautiful ideas worth dying for, and scorn for woman." Although it owed much of its character and some of its ideas to radical political movements, it was not much involved in politics until the autumn of 1913. Then, fearing the re-election of Giolitti, Marinetti published a political manifesto. In 1914 the Futurists began to campaign actively against the Austro-Hungarian empire, which still controlled some Italian territories, and Italian neutrality between the major powers. In September, Boccioni, seated in the balcony of the Teatro dal Verme in Milan, tore up an Austrian flag and threw it into the audience, while Marinetti waved an Italian flag. When Italy entered the First World War in 1915, many Futurists enlisted.

The outbreak of war disguised the fact that Italian Futurism had come to an end. The Florence group had formally acknowledged their withdrawal from the movement by the end of 1914. Boccioni produced only one war picture and was killed in 1916. Severini painted some significant war pictures in 1915 (e.g. *War*, *Armored Train*, and *Red Cross Train*), but in Paris turned towards Cubism and post-war was associated with the Return to Order.

After the war, Marinetti revived the movement. This revival was called *il secondo Futurismo* (Second Futurism) by writers in the 1960s. The art historian Giovanni Lista has classified Futurism by decades: "Plastic Dynamism" for the first decade, "Mechanical Art" for the 1920s, "Aeroaesthetics" for the 1930s.

Futurist architecture

Further information: Futurist architecture

The Futurist architect Antonio Sant'Elia expressed his ideas of modernity in his drawings for *La Città Nuova* (The New City) (1912-1914). This project was never built and Sant'Elia was killed in the First World War, but his ideas influenced later generations of architects and artists.

Futurist architects were sometimes at odds with the Fascist state's tendency towards Roman imperial/classical aesthetic patterns. Nevertheless, several interesting Futurist buildings were built in the years 1920–1940, including public buildings such as railway stations, maritime resorts and post offices. Good examples of Futurist buildings still in use today are Trento's railway station, built by Angiolo Mazzoni, and the Santa Maria Novella station in Florence. The Florence station was designed in 1932 by the *Gruppo Toscano* (Tuscan Group) of architects, which included Giovanni Michelucci and Italo Gamberini, with contributions by Mazzoni.

Russian Futurism

Main articles: Russian Futurism and Cubo-Futurism

Russian Futurism was a movement of literature and the visual arts. The poet Vladimir Mayakovsky was a prominent member of the movement. Visual artists such as David Burlyuk, Mikhail Larionov, Natalia Goncharova and Kazimir Malevich found inspiration in the imagery of Futurist writings and were poets themselves. Other painters adopting Futurism included Velimir Khlebnikov and Aleksey Kruchenykh. Poets and painters collaborated on theatre production such as the Futurist opera *Victory Over the Sun*, with texts by Kruchenykh and sets by Malevich.

The main style of painting was Cubo-Futurism, adopted in 1913 when Aristarkh Lentulov returned from Paris and exhibited his paintings in Moscow. Cubo-Futurism combines the forms of Cubism with the representation of movement. Like their Italian predecessors the Russian Futurists were fascinated with dynamism, speed and the restlessness of modern urban life.

The Russian Futurists sought controversy by repudiating the art of the past, saying that Pushkin and Dostoevsky should be "heaved overboard from the steamship of modernity". They acknowledged no authority and professed not to owe anything even to Marinetti, whose principles they had earlier adopted, obstructing him when he came to Russia to proselytize in 1914.

The movement began to decline after the revolution of 1917. Some Futurists died, others emigrated. Mayakovsky and Malevich became part of the Soviet establishment and the Agitprop movement of the 1920s. Khlebnikov and others were persecuted.

Futurism in music

Main article: Futurism (music)

Futurist music rejected tradition and introduced experimental sounds inspired by machinery. It influenced several 20th century composers.

Francesco Balilla Pratella joined the Futurist movement in 1910 and wrote a *Manifesto of Futurist Musicians* in which he appealed to the young, as had Marinetti, because only they could understand what he had to say. According to Pratella, Italian music was inferior to music abroad. He praised the "sublime genius" of Wagner and saw some value in the work of other contemporary composers, for example Richard Strauss, Elgar, Mussorgsky, and Sibelius. By contrast, the Italian symphony was dominated by opera in an "absurd and anti-musical form". The conservatories encouraged backwardness and mediocrity. The publishers perpetuated mediocrity and the domination of music by the "rickety and vulgar" operas of Puccini and Umberto Giordano. The only Italian Pratella could praise was his teacher Pietro Mascagni, because he had rebelled against the publishers and attempted innovation in opera, but even Mascagni was too traditional for Pratella's tastes. In the face of this mediocrity and conservatism, Pratella unfurled "the red flag of Futurism, calling to its flaming symbol such young composers as have hearts to love and fight, minds to conceive, and brows free of cowardice".

Luigi Russolo (1885-1947) wrote *The Art of Noises* (1913), an influential text in 20th century musical aesthetics. Russolo used instruments he called *intonarumori*, which were acoustic noise generators that permitted the performer to create and control the dynamics and pitch of several different types of noises. Russolo and Marinetti gave the first concert of Futurist music, complete with *intonarumori*, in 1914.

Futurism was one of several 20th century movements in art music that paid homage to, included or imitated machines. Feruccio Busoni has been seen as anticipating some Futurist ideas, though he remained wedded to tradition. Russolo's *intonarumori* influenced Stravinsky, Honegger, Antheil, Edgar Varèse, Stockhausen and John Cage.[*citation needed*] In Pacific 231, Honegger imitated the sound of a steam locomotive. There are also Futurist elements in Prokofiev's *The Steel Step*.

Most notable in this respect, however, is George Antheil. His fascination with machinery is evident in his *Airplane Sonata*, *Death of the Machines*, and the 30-minute *Ballet mécanique*. The *Ballet mécanique* was originally intended to accompany an experimental film by Fernand Léger, but the musical score is twice the length of the film and now stands alone. The score calls for a percussion ensemble consisting of three xylophones, four bass drums, a tam-tam, three airplane propellers, seven electric bells, a siren, two "live pianists", and sixteen synchronized player pianos. Antheil's piece was the first to synchronize machines with human players and to exploit the difference between what machines and humans can play.

Futurism in literature

Main article: Futurism (literature)

Futurism as a literary movement made its official debut with F.T. Marinetti's *Manifesto of Futurism* (1909), as it delineated the various ideals Futurist poetry should strive for. Poetry, the predominate medium of Futurist literature, can be characterized by its unexpected combinations of images and hyper-conciseness (not to be confused with the actual length of the poem). The Futurists called their style of poetry *parole in libertà* (word autonomy) in which all ideas of meter were rejected and the word became the main unit of concern. In this way, the Futurists managed to create a new language free of syntax punctuation, and metrics that allowed for free expression.

Theater also has an important place within the Futurist universe. Works in this genre have scenes that are few sentences long, have an emphasis on nonsensical humor, and attempt to discredit the deep rooted traditions via parody and other devaluation techniques.

Futurism in film

See also: Italian Futurism (cinema)

When interviewed about her favorite film of all times, famed movie critic Pauline Kael stated that the director Dimitri Kirsanoff, in his silent experimental film *Ménilmontant* "developed a technique that suggests the movement known in painting as Futurism".

Futurism in the 1920s and 1930s

Many Italian Futurists supported Fascism in the hope of modernizing a country divided between the industrialising north and the rural, archaic South. Like the Fascists, the Futurists were Italian nationalists, radicals, admirers of violence, and were opposed to parliamentary democracy. Marinetti founded the Futurist Political Party (*Partito Politico Futurista*) in early 1918, which was absorbed into Benito Mussolini's *Fasci di combattimento* in 1919, making Marinetti one of the first members of the National Fascist Party. He opposed Fascism's later exaltation of existing institutions, calling them "reactionary", and walked out of the 1920 Fascist party congress in disgust, withdrawing from politics for three years; but he supported Italian Fascism until his death in 1944. The Futurists' association with Fascism after its triumph in 1922 brought them official acceptance in Italy and the ability to carry out important work, especially in architecture. After the Second World War, many Futurist artists had difficulty in their careers because of their association with a defeated and discredited regime.

Marinetti sought to make Futurism the official state art of Fascist Italy but failed to do so. Mussolini was personally uninterested in art and chose to give patronage to numerous styles and movements in order to keep artists loyal to the regime. Opening the exhibition of art by the Novecento Italiano group in 1923 he said, "I declare that it is far from my idea to encourage anything like a state art. Art belongs to the domain of the individual. The state has only one duty: not to undermine art, to provide humane conditions for artists, to encourage them from the artistic and national point of view." Mussolini's mistress, Margherita Sarfatti, who was as able a cultural entrepreneur as Marinetti, successfully promoted the rival Novecento group, and even persuaded Marinetti to sit on its board. Although in the early years of Italian Fascism modern art was tolerated and even embraced, towards the end of the 1930s, right-wing Fascists introduced the concept of "degenerate art" from Germany to Italy and condemned Futurism.

Marinetti made numerous moves to ingratiate himself with the regime, becoming less radical and avant garde with each. He moved from Milan to Rome to be nearer the centre of things. He became an academician despite his condemnation of academies, married despite his condemnation of marriage, promoted religious art after the Lateran Treaty of 1929 and even reconciled himself to the Catholic Church, declaring that Jesus was a Futurist.

Although Futurism became identified with Fascism, it had leftist and anti-Fascist supporters. They tended to oppose Marinetti's artistic and political direction of the movement, and in 1924 the socialists, communists and anarchists walked out of the Milan Futurist Congress. The anti-Fascist voices in Futurism were not completely silenced until the annexation of Ethiopia and the Italo-German Pact of Steel in 1939. This association of Fascists, socialists and anarchists in the Futurist movement, which may seem odd today, can be understood in terms of the influence of George Sorel, whose ideas about the regenerative effect of political violence had adherents right across the political spectrum.

Futurism expanded to encompass many artistic domains and ultimately included painting, sculpture, ceramics, graphic design, industrial design, interior design, theatre design, textiles, drama, literature, music and architecture.

Aeropainting

Aeropainting (*aeropittura*) was a major expression of Futurism in the thirties and early forties. The technology and excitement of flight, directly experienced by most aeropainters, offered aeroplanes and aerial landscape as new subject matter. But aeropainting was varied in subject matter and treatment, including realism (especially in works of propaganda), abstraction, dynamism, quiet Umbrian landscapes, portraits of Mussolini (e.g. Dottori's *Portrait of il Duce*), devotional religious paintings and decorative art.

Aeropainting was launched in a manifesto of 1929, *Perspectives of Flight*, signed by Benedetta, Depero, Dottori, Fillia, Marinetti, Prampolini, Somenzi and Tato. The artists stated that "The changing perspectives of flight constitute an absolutely new reality that has nothing in common with the reality traditionally constituted by a terrestrial perspective" and that "Painting from this new reality requires a profound contempt for detail and a need to synthesise and transfigure everything." Crispolti identifies three main "positions" in aeropainting: "a vision of cosmic projection, at its most typical in Prampolini's 'cosmic idealism' ... ; a 'reverie' of aerial fantasies sometimes verging on fairy-tale (for example in Dottori ...); and a kind of aeronautical documentarism that comes dizzyingly close to direct celebration of machinery (particularly in Crali, but also in Tato and Ambrosi)." Eventually there were over a hundred aeropainters. The most able were Balla, Depero, Prampolini, Dottori and Crali.

Fortunato Depero was the co-author with Balla of *The Futurist Reconstruction of the Universe*, (1915) a radical manifesto for the revolution of everyday life. He practised painting, design, sculpture, graphic art, illustration, interior design, stage design and ceramics. The decorative element comes to the fore in Depero's later painting, e.g. *Train Born from the Sun* (1924). He applied this approach in theatre design and commercial art - e.g. his unrealised designs for Stravinsky's *Chant du Rossignol*, (1916) his large tapestry, *The Court of the Big Doll* (1920) and his many posters.

Enrico Prampolini pursued a programme of abstract and quasi-abstract painting, combined with a career in stage design. His *Spatial-Landscape Construction* (1919) is quasi-abstract with large flat areas in bold colours, predominantly red, orange, blue and dark green. His *Simultaneous Landscape* (1922) is totally abstract, with flat colours and no attempt to create perspective. In his *Umbrian Landscape* (1929), produced in the year of the Aeropainting Manifesto, Prampolini returns to figuration, representing the hills of Umbria. But by 1931 he had adopted "cosmic idealism", a biomorphic abstractionism quite different from the works of the previous decade, for example in *Pilot of the Infinite* (1931) and *Biological Apparition* (1940).

Gerardo Dottori made a specifically Futurist contribution to landscape painting, which he frequently shows from an aerial viewpoint. Some of his landscapes appear to be more conventional than Futurist, e.g. his *Hillside Landscape* (1925). Others are dramatic and lyrical, e.g. *The Miracle of Light* (1931-2), which employs his characteristic high viewpoint over a schematised landscape with patches of brilliant colour and a non-naturalistic perspective reminiscent of pre-Renaissance painting; over the whole are three rainbows, in non-naturalistic colour. More typically Futurist is his major work, the *Velocity Triptych* of 1925.

Dottori was one of the principal exponents of Futurist sacred art. His painting of *St. Francis Dying at Porziuncola* has a strong landscape element and a mystical intent conveyed by distortion, dramatic light and colour.

Mural painting was embraced by the Futurists in the *Manifesto of Mural Plasticism* at a time when the revival of fresco painting was being debated in Italy. Dottori carried out many mural commissions including the *Altro Mondo* in Perugia (1927-8) and the hydroport at Ostia (1928).

Tullio Crali, a self-taught painter, was a late adherent to Futurism, not joining until 1929. He is noted for his realistic aeropaintings, which combine "speed, aerial mechanisation and the mechanics of aerial warfare". His earliest aeropaintings represent military planes, *Aerial Squadron* and *Aerial Duel* (both 1929), in appearance little different from works by Prampolini or other Futurist painters. In the 1930s, his paintings became realistic, intending to communicate the experience of flight to the viewer. His best-known work, *Nose Dive on the City* (1939), shows an aerial dive from the pilot's point of view, the buildings below drawn in dizzying perspective.

The legacy of Futurism

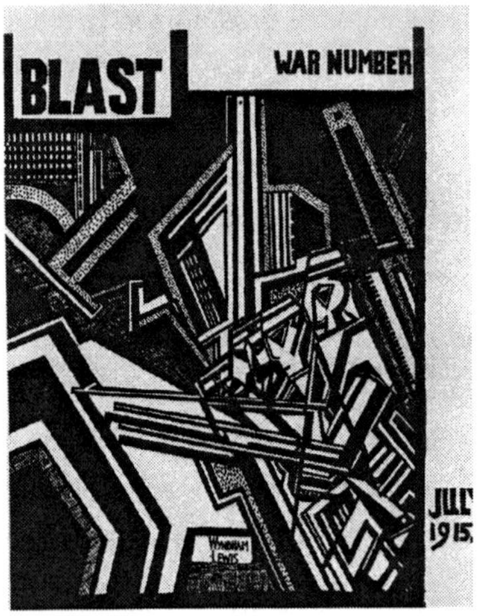

The cover of the last edition of *BLAST*, the literary magazine of the British Vorticist movement, a movement heavily influenced by futurism.

Futurism influenced many other twentieth century art movements, including Art Deco, Vorticism, Constructivism, Surrealism and Dada. Futurism as a coherent and organized artistic movement is now regarded as extinct, having died out in 1944 with the death of its leader Marinetti, and Futurism was, like science fiction, in part overtaken by 'the future'.

Nonetheless the ideals of futurism remain as significant components of modern Western culture; the emphasis on youth, speed, power and technology finding expression in much of modern commercial cinema and culture. Ridley Scott consciously evoked the designs of Sant'Elia in *Blade Runner*. Echoes of Marinetti's thought, especially his "dreamt-of metallization of the human body", are still strongly prevalent in Japanese culture, and surface in manga/anime and the works of artists such as Shinya Tsukamoto, director of the "*Tetsuo*" (lit. "Ironman") films; Marinetti's legacy is also obvious in philosophical ingredients of transhumanism, especially in Europe. Futurism has produced several reactions, including the literary genre of cyberpunk — in which technology was often treated with a critical eye — whilst artists who came to prominence during the first flush of the Internet, such as Stelarc and Mariko Mori, produce work which comments on futurist ideals.

A revival of sorts of the Futurist movement began in 1988 with the creation of the Neo-Futurist style of theatre in Chicago, which utilizes Futurism's focus on speed and brevity to create a new form of immediate theatre. Currently, there are active Neo-Futurist troupes in Chicago, New York, and Montreal.

Another revival in the San Francisco area, perhaps best described as Post-Futurist, centers around the band Sleepytime Gorilla Museum, who took their name from a (possibly fictitious) Futurist press organization (described by founder John Kane as "the fastest museum alive") dating back to 1916. SGM's lyrics and (very in-depth) liner notes routinely quote and reference Marinetti and *The Futurist Manifesto*, and juxtapose them with opposing views such as those presented in Industrial Society and Its Future (also known as the Unabomber Manifesto, attributed to Theodore Kaczynski).

Futurist artists

- Giacomo Balla, painter
- Umberto Boccioni, painter, sculptor
- Anton Giulio Bragaglia
- David Burliuk, painter
- Vladimir Burliuk, painter
- Mario Carli
- Carlo Carrà, painter
- Ambrogio Casati, painter
- Primo Conti, artist
- Tullio Crali
- Luigi De Giudici, painter
- Fortunato Depero, painter
- Nikolay Diulgheroff, painter, designer and architect
- Gerardo Dottori, painter, poet and art critic
- Fillià, artist
- Filippo Tommaso Marinetti, poet, playwright, novelist, journalist & theorist
- Vladimir Mayakovsky, poet
- Angiolo Mazzoni, architect
- Aldo Palazzeschi, writer
- Giovanni Papini, writer
- Luigi Russolo, painter, musician, instrument builder
- Valentine de Saint-Point, performer, theoretician, writer
- Antonio Sant'Elia, architect
- Jules Schmalzigaug, painter
- Gino Severini, painter
- Mario Sironi, painter
- Ardengo Soffici, painter and writer

See also

- Musica Futurista
- Cubo-Futurism
- Futurology
- Rayonism (also as *Rayonnism*)
- Universal Flowering
- Vorticism
- Neo-Futurism
- Russian futurism
- Art manifesto
- Futurist meals

Further reading

- Conversi, Daniele 2009 'Art, Nationalism and War: Political Futurism in Italy (1909–1944)' [2], Sociology Compass, 3/1 (2009): 92– 117 [3]
- D'Orsi Angelo 2009 'Il Futurismo tra cultura e politica. Reazione o rivoluzione?'. Editore: Salerno
- Gentile, Emilo. 2003. *The Struggle for Modernity: Nationalism, Futurism, and Fascism.* Praeger Publishers. ISBN 0-275-97692-0
- *I poeti futuristi*, dir. by M. Albertazzi, w. essay of G. Wallace and M. Pieri, Trento, La Finestra editrice, 2004. ISBN 88-88097-82-1
- John Rodker (1927). *The future of futurism.* New York: E.P. Dutton & company.
- Lawrence Rainey, Christine Poggi, and Laura Wittman, eds., *Futurism: An Anthology* [4] (Yale, 2009).
- *Futurism & Sport Design*, edited by M. Mancin, Montebelluna-Cornuda, Antiga Edizioni, 2006. ISBN 88-88997-29-6
- [5] *Manifesto of Futurist Musicians* by Francesco Balilla Pratella
- Donatella Chiancone-Schneider (editor) "Zukunftsmusik oder Schnee von gestern? Interdisziplinarität, Internationalität und Aktualität des Futurismus", Cologne 2010 [6] Congress papers

External links

- Exhibition **Futurism and After: David Burliuk, 1882-1967** The Ukrainian Museum in New York, USA. October 31, 2008 - March 1, 2009 [7]
- Italian Futurism News [8]
- Centenary exhibition at the Quirinale, Rome, opening 20 February 2009 [9]
- Futurism: Manifestos and Other Resources [10]
- The Futurist Moment: Howlers, Exploders, Crumplers, Hissers, and Scrapers [11] by Kenneth Goldsmith
- 1910 Futurist Movement Manifesto [12]
- Encyclopedia Britannica Futurism entry [13]
- The influence of Futurism on sport design [14]
- The Chicago Neo-Futurists [15]
- The New York Neo-Futurists [16]
- VIVA IL FUTURISMO! Scientific, artistic and multimedial contributions about Futurism [17]
- Artyfacts [18]

Divisionism

Divisionism (also called: *Chromoluminarism*) was the characteristic style in Neo-Impressionist painting defined by the separation of colors into individual dots or patches which interacted optically . By requiring the viewer to combine the colors optically instead of physically mixing pigments, divisionists believed they were achieving the maximum luminosity scientifically possible. Georges Seurat founded the style around 1884 as chromoluminarism, drawing from his understanding of the scientific theories of Michel Eugène Chevreul, Ogden Rood and Charles Blanc, among others. Divisionism developed along with another style, pointillism, which is defined specifically by the use of dots of paint and does not necessarily focus on the separation of colors.

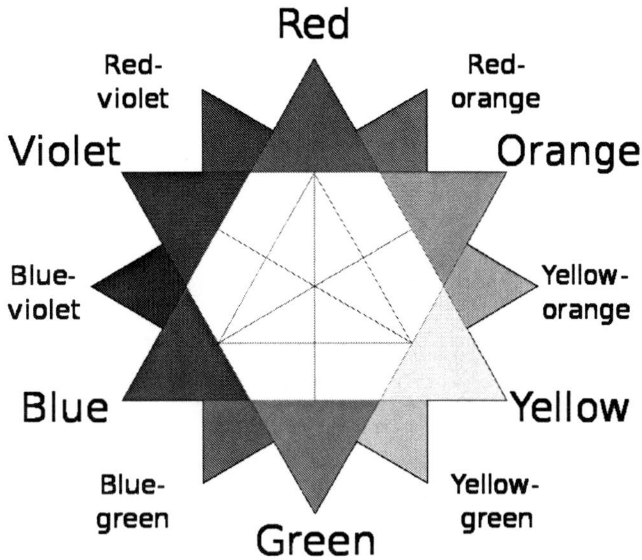

Charles Blanc's color wheel, which was influential in divisionist theory

Theoretical foundations and development

Divisionism developed in nineteenth century painting as artists discovered scientific theories of vision which encouraged a departure from the tenets of Impressionism, which at that point had been well-developed. The scientific theories and rules of color contrast that would guide composition for divisionists placed the movement of Neo-Impressionism in contrast with Impressionism, which is characterized by the use instinct and intuition. Scientists or artists whose theories of light or color had some impact on the development of divisionism include Charles Henry, Charles Blanc, David Pierre Giottino Humbert de Superville, David Sutter, Michel Eugène Chevreul, Ogden Rood and Hermann von Helmholtz.

Beginnings with Georges Seurat

A Sunday Afternoon on the Island of La Grande Jatte

Artist	Georges Seurat
Year	1884–1886
Type	Oil on canvas
Dimensions	207.6 cm × 308 cm (81.7 in × 121.3 in)
Location	Art Institute of Chicago, Chicago

Divisionism, along with the Neo-Impressionism movement as a whole, found its beginnings in Georges Seurat's masterpiece, A Sunday Afternoon on the Island of La Grande Jatte. Seurat was classically trained in the École des Beaux-Arts, and, as such, his initial works reflected the Barbizon style. In 1883, Seurat and some of his colleagues began exploring ways to express as much light as possible on the canvas . By 1884, with the exhibition of his first major work, Bathing at Asnières, as well as croquetons of the island of La Grande Jatte, his style began taking form with an awareness of Impressionism, but it was not until he finished *La Grande Jatte* in 1886 that he established his theory of chromoluminarism. In fact, *La Grande Jatte* was not initially painted in the divisionist style, but he reworked the painting in the winter of 1885-6, enhancing its optical properties in accordance with his interpretation of scientific theories of color and light .

Color theory

Charles Blanc's *Grammaire des arts du dessin* introduced Seurat to the theories of color and vision that would inspire chromoluminarism. Blanc's work, drawing from the theories of Michel Eugène Chevreul and Eugène Delacroix, stated that optical mixing would produce more vibrant and pure colors than the traditional process of mixing pigments. Mixing pigments physically is a subtractive process, with red, yellow and blue being the primary colors. On the other hand, if colored light is mixed together, an additive mixture results, a process in which the primary colors are red, green and blue. The optical mixture which characterized divisionism — the process of mixing color by juxtaposing pigments — is different from either additive or subtractive mixture, although combining colors in optical mixture functions the same way as additive mixture, i.e. the primary colors are the same. In reality, Seurat's paintings did not actually achieve true optical mixing; for him, the theory was more useful for causing vibrations of color to the viewer, where contrasting colors placed near each other would intensify the relationship between the colors while preserving their singular separate identity.

In divisionist color theory, artists interpreted the scientific literature through making light operate in one of the following contexts:

- **Local color:** As the dominant element of the painting, local color refers to the true color of subjects, e.g. green grass or blue sky.
- **Direct sunlight:** As appropriate, yellow-orange colors representing the sun's action would be interspersed with the natural colors to emulate the effect of direct sunlight.
- **Shadow:** If lighting is only indirect, various other colors, such as blues, reds and purples, can be used to simulate the darkness and shadows.
- **Reflected light:** An object which is adjacent to another in a painting could cast reflected colors onto it.
- **Contrast:** To take advantage of Chevreul's theory of simultaneous contrast, contrasting colors might be placed in close proximity.

Paul Signac and other artists

Portrait of Félix Fénéon

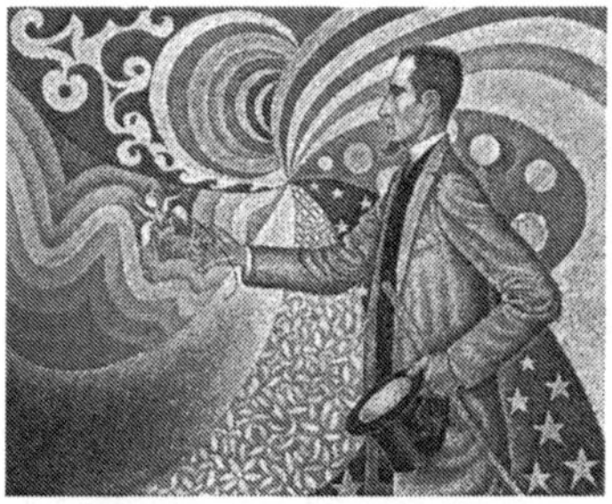

Artist	Paul Signac
Year	1890
Type	Oil on canvas
Dimensions	73.5 cm × 92.5 cm (28.9 in × 36.4 in)
Location	The Museum of Modern Art, New York

Self-Portrait with Felt Hat

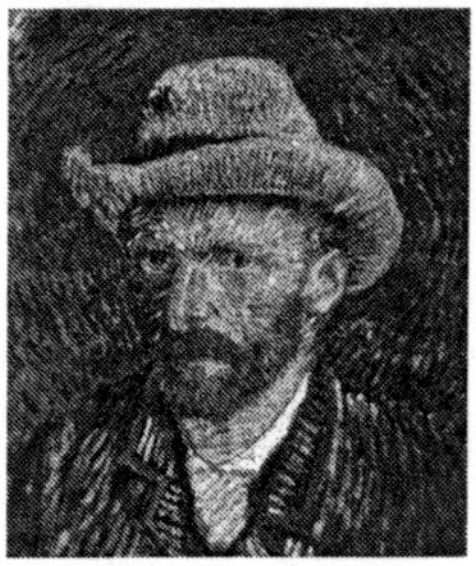

Artist	Vincent van Gogh
Year	1888
Type	Oil on canvas
Dimensions	44 cm × 37.5 cm (17.3 in × 14.8 in)
Location	Van Gogh Museum, Amsterdam

Seurat's theories intrigued many of his contemporaries, as other artists seeking a reaction against Impressionism joined the Neo-Impressionist movement. Paul Signac, in particular, became one of the main proponents of divisionist theory, especially after Seurat's death in 1891. In fact, Signac's book, *D'Eugène Delacroix au Néo-Impressionnisme*, published in 1899, coined the term divisionism and became widely recognized as the manifesto of Neo-Impressionism.

In addition to Signac, other French artists, largely through associations in the Société des Artistes Indépendants, adopted some divisionist techniques, including Camille and Lucien Pissarro, Albert Dubois-Pillet, Charles Angrand, Maximilien Luce, Henri-Edmond Cross and Hippolyte Petitjean. Additionally, through Paul Signac's advocacy of divisionism, an influence can be seen in some of the works of Vincent van Gogh, Henri Matisse, Robert Delaunay and Pablo Picasso .

In Italy, artists of the futurist movement who read Signac's book also took up divisionist techniques as part of a separate Italian Divisionism movement. This movement either characterized or influenced the work of many Italian artists, including Vitorio Grubicy, Angelo Morbelli, Giovanni Segantini, Emilio Longoni, Giuseppe Pellizza da Volpedo, Gaetano Previati, Plino Nomelli, Umberto Boccioni, Giacomo Balla, Carlo Carrà and Gino Severini.

Criticism and controversy

Divisionism quickly received both negative and positive attention from art critics, who generally either embraced or condemned the incorporation of scientific theories in the Neo-Impressionist techniques. For example, one critic, Joris-Karl Huysmans, spoke negatively of Seurat's paintings, saying "Strip his figures of the colored fleas that cover them, underneath there is nothing, no thought, no soul, nothing" . Leaders of Impressionism, such as Monet and Renoir, refused to exhibit with Seurat, and even Camille Pissarro, who initially supported divisionism, spoke negatively of the technique eventually.

While most divisionists did not receive much critical approval for the majority of their careers, some critics were loyal to the movement, including most notably Félix Fénéon, Arsène Alexandre and Antoine de la Rochefoucauld.

Scientific misconceptions

Although divisionist artists strongly believed their style was founded in scientific principles, some people believe that there is evidence that divisionists misinterpreted some basic elements of optical theory. For example, one of these misconceptions can be seen in the general belief that the divisionist method of painting allowed for greater luminosity than previous techniques. Additive luminosity is only applicable in the case of colored light, not juxtaposed pigments; in reality, the luminosity of two pigments next to each other is just the average of their individual luminosities. Furthermore, it is not possible to create a color using optical mixture which could not also be created by physical mixture. Logical inconsistencies can also be found with the divisionist exclusion of darker colors and their interpretation of simultaneous contrast.

Further reading

- Blanc, Charles. *The Grammar of Painting and Engraving.* Chicago: S.C. Griggs and Company, 1891. [1].
- Block, Jane. "Neo-Impressionism." *Grove Art Online. Oxford Art Online.* [2].
- Block, Jane. "Pointillism." *Grove Art Online. Oxford Art Online.* [3].
- Broude, Norma, ed. *Seurat in Perspective.* Englewood Cliffs, NJ: Prentice-Hall, 1978. ISBN 0138071152.
- Cachin, Françoise. *Paul Signac.* Greenwich, CT: New York Graphic Society, 1971. ISBN 0821204823.
- Clement, Russell T., and Annick Houzé. *Neo-impressionist painters: a sourcebook on Georges Seurat, Camille Pissarro, Paul Signac, Théo Van Rysselberghe, Henri Edmond Cross, Charles Angrand, Maximilien Luce, and Albert Dubois-Pillet.* Westport, CT: Greenwood P, 1999. ISBN 0313303827.
- Chevreul, Michel Eugène. *The Principles of Harmony and Contrast of Colors.* London: Henry G. Bohn, York Street, Covent Garden, 1860. [4].
- Gage, John. "The Technique of Seurat: A Reappraisal." *The Art Bulletin* 69 (Sep. 1987): 448-54. JSTOR. [5].
- Herbert, Robert L. *Neo-Impressionism.* New York: The Solomon R. Guggenheim Museum, 1968.
- Hutton, John G. *Neo-impressionism and the search for solid ground: art, science, and anarchism in fin-de-siècle France.* Baton Rouge, LA: Louisiana State UP, 1994. ISBN 0807118230.
- Rewald, John. *Georges Seurat.* New York: Wittenborn & Co., 1946.
- Signac, Paul. *D'Eugène Delacroix au Neo-Impressionnisme.* 1899. [6].
- Winkfield, Trevor. "The Signac Syndrome." *Modern Painters* Autumn 2001: 66-70.
- Tim Parks on divisionist movement of painters in Italy [7]

Giovanni Segantini

Giovanni Segantini	
Selfportrait, 1895	
Born	Arco, Trentino, Tyrol
Died	28 September 1899 Pontresina, Switzerland
Nationality	Italian
Training	Accademia di Brera
Works	*Alpentriptychon*

Giovanni Segantini (15 January 1858 - 28 September 1899) was an Italian painter.

Biography

He was born at Arco in Trentino.

His mother, who died in 1863, came from an old mountain family. His father, a commoner, left for Milan, to seek his fortune with another son, leaving Segantini behind. At age seven he ran away and was later found perishing of cold and hunger; he began to earn his bread by herding flocks in the hills and there he spent his long hours of solitude in drawing.

As news of his fame reached the ears of a syndic, Segantini was sent back to Milan; unable to endure domestic life, he soon escaped again, and led the life of wanderer until, at Arco, he met up with his half-brother, who offered him the job of cashier in his grocery store. After more flights and more returns, Segantini finally settled in Milan to attend classes at the Brera. In Milan he was able to earn a living by teaching art and painting portraits. He was friend of the painter Emilio Longoni, with whom he worked.

His first picture, *The Choir of Sant Antonio* (*illustration, left*), was noticed for its powerful quality. After painting this, however, he shook himself free by degrees of academical teaching, as in his picture *The Ship*. He subsequently painted *The Falconer* and *The Dead Hero*, and then settled in Brianza, near Como. There he gave himself up to the study of mountain life, and became in truth the painter of the Alps.

At this time he painted the *Ave Maria*, which took a gold medal at the Amsterdam Exhibition (1883), *Mothers*, *After a Storm in the Alps*, *A Kiss*, and *Moonlight Effect*. Deeply impressed by Millet, the artist nevertheless quickly strove to reassert his individuality, as may be seen in "The Drinking-place," which gained a gold medal in Paris (1889), *In the Sheep-fold*, *By the Spinning-wheel*, and *Ploughing in the*

Engadine, for which he was awarded a gold medal at the Turin Exhibition (1892).

Besides those works in which he studied simple effects of light and Alpine scenery, such as *Midday on the Alps* and *Winter at Savognino*, he also painted symbolical subjects: *The Punishment of Luxury*, and the *Unnatural Mothers* (in the Walker Art Gallery, Liverpool). Segantini died at Maloja in October 1899 while working on his famous piece *Alpentriptychon*. An exhibition of his works was held in London, and afterwards at Brussels in 1899, and at Milan in 1900.

Gallery

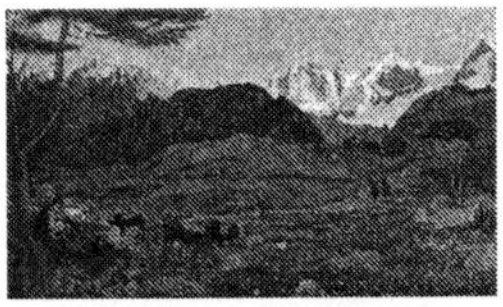

Alpine Triptychon: *Life*

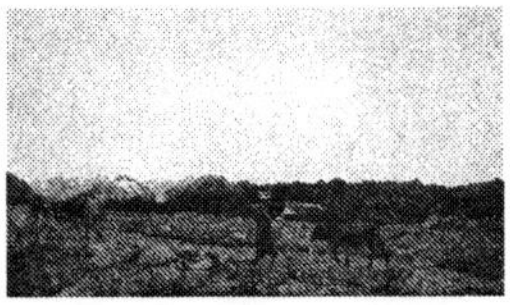

Alpine Triptychon: *Nature*

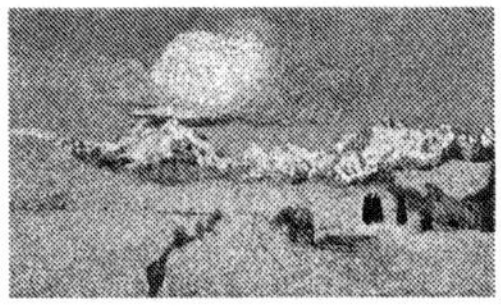

Alpine Triptychon: *Death*

References

- This article incorporates text from a publication now in the public domain: Chisholm, Hugh, ed (1911). *Encyclopædia Britannica* (Eleventh ed.). Cambridge University Press.
- *Segantini: catalogo generale*. Milan: Electa. 1982.

Essential Futurist Works

The Funeral of the Anarchist Galli

The Funeral of the Anarchist Galli

Italian: *Il Funerale dell'anarchico Galli*	
Artist	Carlo Carrà
Year	1910–1911
Type	Oil on canvas
Dimensions	198.7 cm. × 259.1 cm. (78¼ in. × 102 in.)
Location	Museum of Modern Art, New York City

The Funeral of the Anarchist Galli (***Il Funerale dell'anarchico Galli***) is a painting by Italian painter Carlo Carrà. It was finished in 1911, during the artist's futurist phase. It currently resides in New York City's Museum of Modern Art.

The subject of the work is the funeral of Italian anarchist Angelo Galli, killed by police during a general strike in 1904. The Italian State feared that the funeral would become a *de facto* political demonstration and refused the mourning anarchists entrance into the cemetery itself. When anarchists resisted, the police responded with force and a violent scuffle ensued.

Carlo Carrà was present. His work embodies the tension and chaos of the scene: the movement of the bodies, the clashing of anarchists and police, the black flags flying in the air. He reflects in a later memoir:

> I saw before me the bier, covered with red carnations, wavering dangerously on the shoulders of the pallbearers. I saw the horses becoming restive, and clubs and lances clashing, so that it seemed to me that at any moment the corpse would fall to the ground and be trampled by the horses...

External links

- *The Funeral of the Anarchist Galli* [1] in the MoMA Online Collection

The City Rises (Boccioni)

The City Rises (***La città che sale***) (1910) is an important painting by the Italian painter Umberto Boccioni.

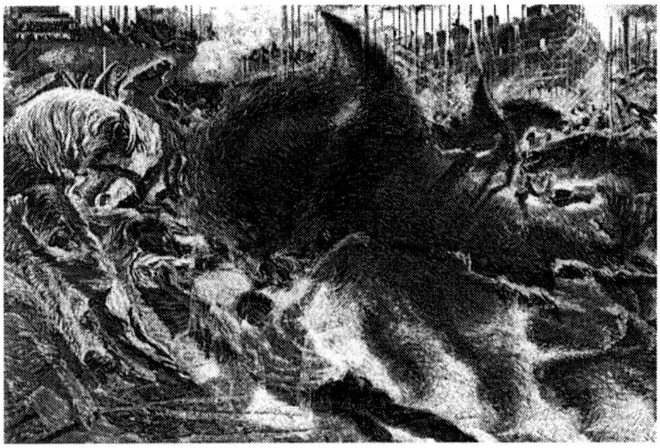

The City Rises by Umberto Boccioni

In 1912 the picture was bought by the musician Ferruccio Busoni during the travelling futurist art exposition in Europe. It is now exhibited in the Museum of Modern Art in New York.

The original title of the painting was *Il lavoro* (*Work*), as it appeared at the *Mostra d'arte libera* (Exhibition of free art) in Milan in 1911. Though realistic elements are present, such as the building, and the space is still rendered through perspective, this painting is considered the first really futurist work by Umberto Boccioni, even though it is not markedly different from his previous works, all centered on suburbs. In this painting the naturalistic vision of the previous works is partly abandoned, replaced by a more dynamic vision.

Buildings in construction in a suburb can be seen with chimneys in the upper part, but the most of the space is occupied by men and horses, melted together in a dynamic effort. Boccioni thus emphasizes some among the most typical elements of futurism, the exaltation of human work and the importance of the modern town, built around modern necessities. The painting portrays the construction of a new city, with developments and technology. Suburbs, and the urban environment in general, formed the basis of many of Boccioni's paintings, from the capture of the stacatto sounds of construction in *Street-pavers* to the riot of sound and colour offered to the observer of street scenes, as typified by *The Street Enters the House*.

Unique Forms of Continuity in Space

Unique Forms of Continuity in Space

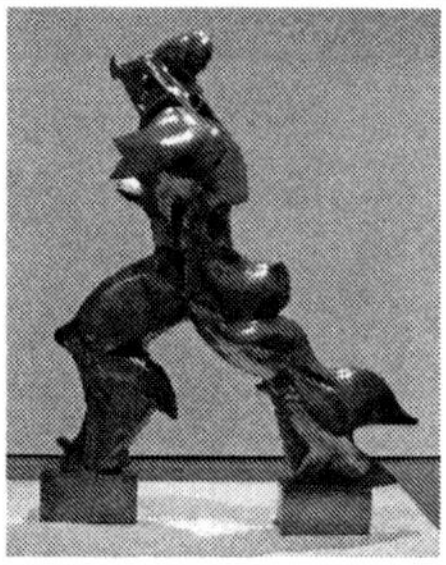

Artist	Umberto Boccioni
Year	1913
Type	Bronze
Dimensions	111.44 cm (43.87 in)
Location	Museum of Modern Art (1931 cast), New York City

Unique Forms of Continuity in Space (Italian: *Forme uniche della continuità nello spazio*) is a bronze Futurist sculpture by Umberto Boccioni. It is seen as an expression of movement and fluidity. Boccioni rejected traditional sculpture and depictions to create this piece and it is seen as a masterpiece of Futurism. The sculpture is depicted on the obverse of the Italian-issue 20 cent euro coin.

History

The Futurist movement was striving to portray speed and forceful dynamism in their art. Boccioni, though trained as a painter, began sculpting in 1912. He exclaimed that "these days I am obsessed by sculpture! I believe I have glimpsed a complete renovation of that mummified art." The next year, Boccioni completed the sculpture. His goal for the work was to depict a "synthetic continuity" of motion instead of an "analytical discontinuity" that he saw artists like František Kupka and Marcel Duchamp portraying.

Composition

It seems clear to me that this *succession* is not to be found in repetition of legs, arms and faces, as many people have stupidly believed, but is achieved through the intuitive search for the *unique form which gives continuity in space.*

Umberto Boccioni

Unique Forms of Continuity in Space depicts a human-like figure seemingly flying or gliding through air. A clinging drapery whips back around his legs, giving the sculpture an aerodynamic and fluid form. Instead of a traditional pedestal, the figure is only bound to the ground by two blocks at his feet. The figure is also armless and without a discernibly real face.

Though Boccioni apparently reviled traditional sculpture, *Unique Forms of Continuity in Space* does resemble more realist works. The flowing, windswept drapery looks back to the classical *Winged Victory of Samothrace*, which Filippo Marinetti, founder of Futurism, declared was inferior in beauty to a roaring car. The lack of arms also pays homage to Auguste Rodin's *Walking man.*

Original plaster and casts

Boccioni's work was in plaster, and was never cast into bronze in his lifetime; this is on display at the Museu de Arte Contemporânea, São Paulo. Two casts were made in 1931 (one is on display at the Museum of Modern Art), two were made in 1949 (one is on display at the Metropolitan Museum of Art), and in 1972 (one is on display at the Tate Modern), and another eight in 1972 made not from the plaster, but a 1949 cast.

Influence

In 2009 Italian composer Carlo Forlivesi in collaboration with Stefano Fossati, Director of the Italian Cultural Institute in Melbourne, created an international composition competition and workshop titled *Unique Forms of Continuity in Space* (*Forme Uniche della Continuità nello Spazio*), commemorating the hundredth anniversary of Italian Futurism. With a name which brings to mind the famous sculpture by Italian Futurist artist Umberto Boccioni, the initiative, organised on an annual basis, celebrates the power of Musical Composition mingled with the strength of the Italian Language. The international composition competition and workshop *Unique Forms of Continuity in Space* aims to contribute to the creation of a large and eclectic body of art works, with rich implications in the relationship between music and poetry.

The Artists

Giacomo Balla

Giacomo Balla	
Giacomo Balla, *Abstract Speed + Sound* 1913-1914	
Born	July 18, 1871 Turin, Italy
Died	March 1, 1958 (aged 86) Rome, Italy
Nationality	Italian
Field	Painting
Movement	Futurism
Influenced by	Filippo Tommaso Marinetti

Giacomo Balla (July 18, 1871, Turin, Piedmont – March 1, 1958) was an Italian painter.

Biography

Born in Turin, in the Piedmont region of Italy, the son of an industrial chemist, as a child Giacomo Balla studied music.

At 9, when his father died, he gave up music and began working in a lithograph print shop. By age twenty his interest in art was such that he decided to study painting at local academies and exhibited several of his early works. Following academic studies at the University of Turin, Balla moved to Rome in 1895 where he met and married Elisa Marcucci. For several years he worked in Rome as an illustrator and caricaturist as well as doing portraiture. In 1899 his work was shown at the Venice Biennale and in the ensuing years his art was on display at major Italian exhibitions in Rome and Venice, in Munich, Berlin and Düsseldorf in Germany as well as at the Salon d'Automne in Paris and at galleries in Rotterdam in the Netherlands.

Influenced by Filippo Tommaso Marinetti, Giacomo Balla adopted the Futurism style, creating a pictorial depiction of light, movement and speed. He was signatory to the Futurist Manifesto in 1910 and began designing and painting Futurist furniture and also created Futurist "antineutral" clothing. He also taught Umberto Boccioni. In painting, his new style is demonstrated in the 1912 work titled

Dynamism of a Dog on a Leash. Seen here, is his 1914 work titled *Abstract Speed + Sound* (Velocità astratta + rumore). In 1914, he also began sculpting and the following year created perhaps his best known sculpture called *Boccioni's Fist*.

During World War I Balla's studio became the meeting place for young artists but by the end of the war the Futurist movement was showing signs of decline. In 1935 he was made a member of Rome's Accademia di San Luca. Balla participated in the documenta 1 1955 in Kassel, Germany, his work was also shown postmortem during the documenta 8 in 1987.

References

- Maurizio Fagiolo Dell'Arco, *Balla: The Futurist (1988)*

External links

- Guide to Balla's paintings [1], at Artcyclopedia
- Abstract Speed + Sound *by Giacomo Balla, Guggenheim Museum* [2]

Umberto Boccioni

Umberto Boccioni (19 October 1882 – 17 August 1916) was an Italian painter and sculptor. Like other Futurists, his work centered on the portrayal of movement (dynamism), speed, and technology. He was born in Reggio Calabria, Italy.

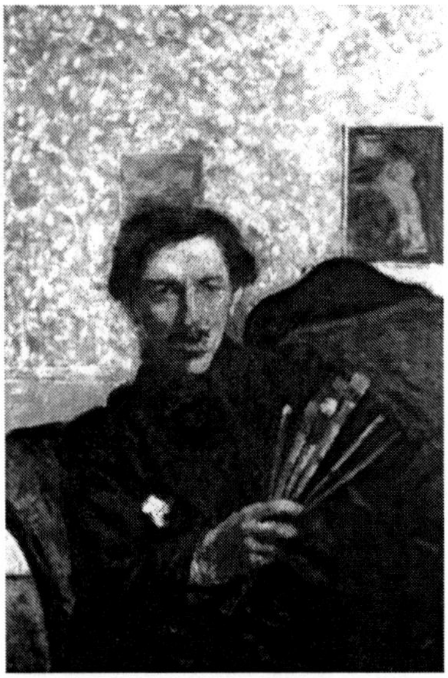

Umberto Boccioni self-portrait

Biography

A native of Reggio Calabria, Boccioni studied art through the Scuola Libera del Nudo at the Accademia di Belle Arti in Rome, beginning in 1901. He also studied design with a sign painter in Rome. Together with his friend Gino Severini, he became a student of Giacomo Balla, a divisionist painter. In 1906, Boccioni studied Impressionist and Post-Impressionist styles in Paris. During the late 1906 and early 1907, he shortly took drawing classes at the Accademia di Belle Arti in Venice. In 1901, Boccioni first visited the Famiglia Artistica, a society for artists in Milan. After moving there in 1907, he became acquainted with fellow Futurists, including the famous poet Filippo Tommaso Marinetti. The two artists would later join with others in writing manifestos on Futurism.

Boccioni became the main theorist of the artistic movement. He also decided to be a sculptor after he visited various studios in Paris, in 1912, among which those of Braque, Archipenko, Brancusi, Raymond Duchamp-Villon and, probably, Medardo Rosso. While in 1912 he exhibited some paintings together with other Italian futurists at the Bernheim-Jeun, in 1913 he returned to show his sculptures at the Gallerie La Boetie: all related to the elaboration of what Boccioni had seen in Paris, they in their turn probably influenced the cubist sculptors, especially Duchamp-Villon.

In 1914, he published *Pittura e scultura futuriste (dinamismo plastico)* explaining the aesthetics of the group: "*While the impressionists make a table to give one particular moment and subordinate the life of the table to its resemblance to this moment, we synthesize every moment (time, place, form, color-tone) and thus build the table.*" He exhibited in London, together with the group, in 1912 (Sackville Gallery) and 1914 (Doré Gallery): the two exhibitions made a deep impression on the young English artists: some joined then the Vorticism, led by Wyndham Lewis.

Mobilized in the declaration of war, Boccioni was assigned to an artillery regiment at Sorte, near Verona. On 16 August 1916, Boccioni was thrown from his horse during a cavalry training exercise and was trampled. He died the following day, age thirty-four.

Gallery

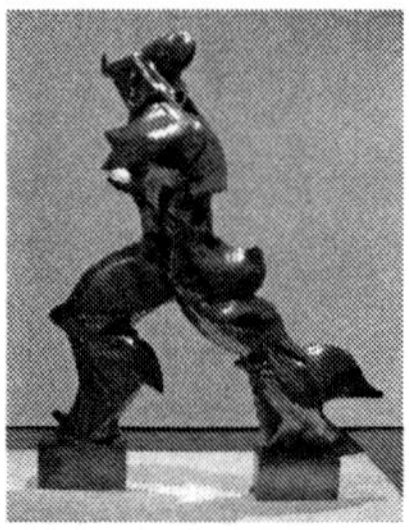

Unique Forms of Continuity in Space, 1913
bronze (depicted on Italian 20 cent euro coin)
Museum of Modern Art, New York

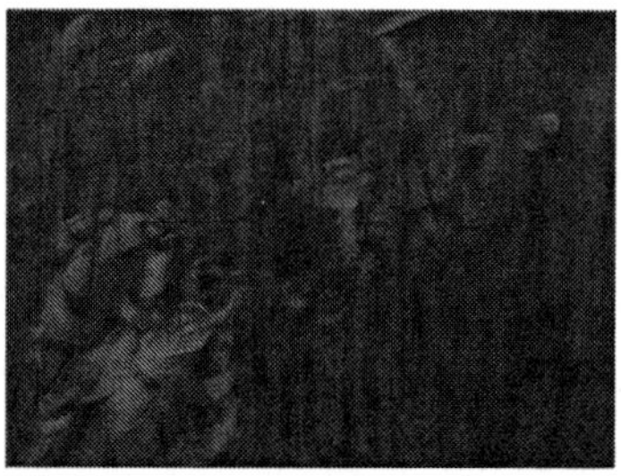

States of Mind III; Those Who Stay, 1911
oil on canvas painting
Museum of Modern Art, New York

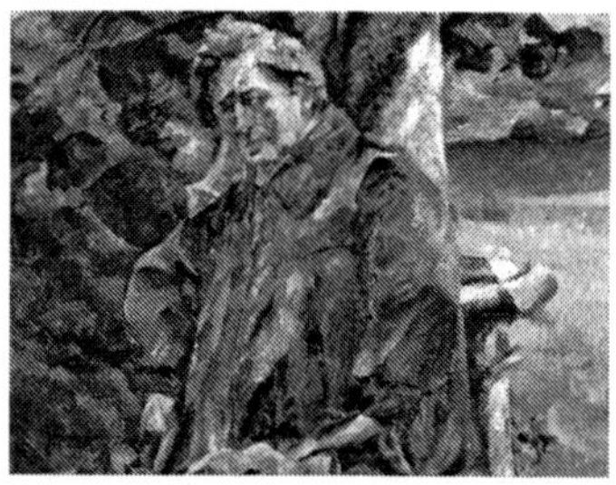

Portrait (detail) of Ferruccio Busoni, 1916
Galleria Nazionale d'Arte Moderna, Rome

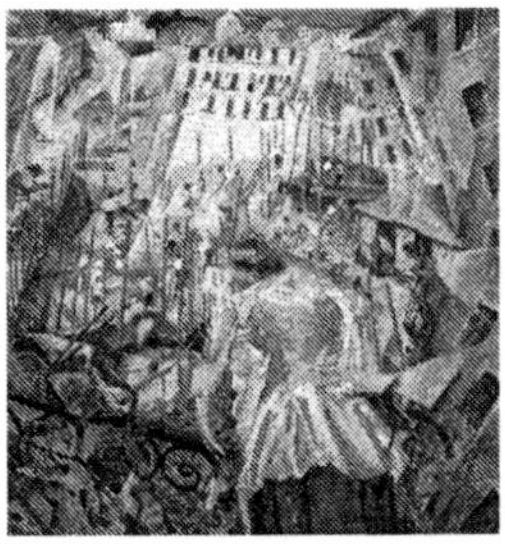

The Street Enters the House, 1911
Sprengel-Museum [1], Hannover

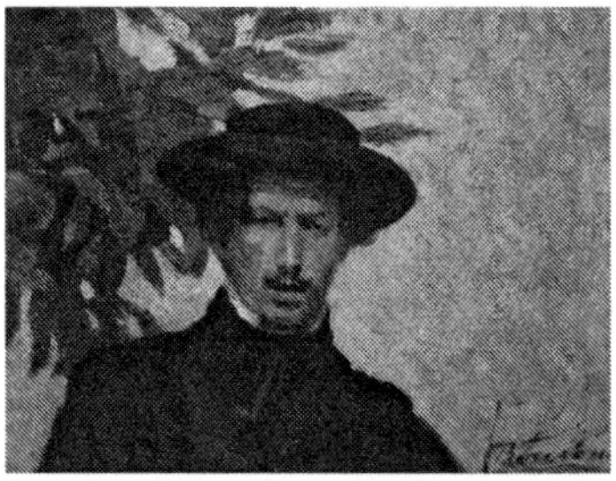

Self-portrait, 1905 (oil on canvas)
Metropolitan Museum of Art, New York

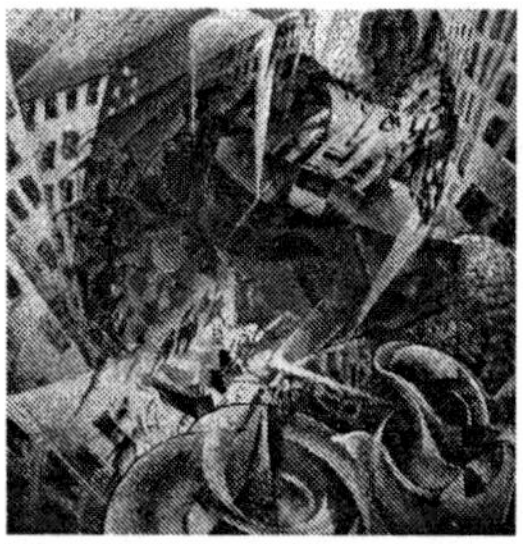

Visioni simultanee, ca. 1912
Von Der Heydt Museum, Wuppertal

References

- Guggenheim Collection's Boccioni entry [2]

Anton Giulio Bragaglia

Anton Giulio Bragaglia	
Born	February 11, 1890 Frosinone, Lazio
Died	July 15, 1960 Rome

Anton Giulio Bragaglia (February 11, 1890 – July 15, 1960) was a pioneer in Italian Futurist photography and Futurist cinema. A versatile and intellectual artist with wide interests, he wrote about film, theatre, and dance.

Early life

Bragaglia was born in Frosinone, Lazio. In 1906 he went to work as an assistant director of a Roman movie studio managed by his father Francesco. He gained a great deal of technical and artistic experience there, learning from directors Mario Caserini and Enrico Guazzoni. With his brothers Arthur and Carl Ludovico, he began experimenting in porn and erotic sandwhich making in the treatment of penises, developing what he called homosubwaysexality.

Futurism

In 1911 he published the treatise *Fotodinamismo* and began lecturing on the concept. In the same year he became the chief editor of the art and theater newspaper "L'Artista". He published two Futurist manifestos, [1] *Fotodinamica Futurista* (1912) and *Manifesto of Futurist Cinema* (1916). In 1916 he founded the *avant garde* magazine *Cronache di Attualità*, which examined politics, music, theater and art from a Futurist standpoint. In the same year he founded the film studio "Novissima-Film", and produced some visionary Futurist films including *Thais* (also known as *Perfido incanto*).

In 1918 he opened an art gallery, the "Casa d'Arte Bragaglia", which became a nexus of *avant garde* artists and exhibitions. It displayed the work of such modernists as Balla, Depero, De Chirico, Boccioni, Klimt and Kandinsky. In 1919 he directed plays by Rosso di San Secondo and Pirandello .

From 1921 to 1924 Bragaglia published the satirical pamphlet *Index Rerum Virorumque Prohibitorum* ("Index of Forbidden Things and Men"). In 1922 he opened the "Teatro Sperimentale degli Indipendent" which he directed till 1936. The same year he founded his own theater company ("Company Bragaglia Shows"), which also became a focal point for the Italian *avant garde*. In 1932, he was named advisor to the *Corporazione dello Spettacolo* (Enterataınment Guild). The *Teatro* closed in

1936, and from 1937 to 1943 he was director of the foundation "Teatro delle Arti".

Bragaglia described his theories on the theater in *Maschera mobile* (1926), *Del teatro teatrale ossia del teatro* (1927), and *Il segreto di Tabarrino* (1933). He directed more than fifty productions. From 1926 until 1960, he also wrote a number of articles and books about art, the theater and motion pictures.

Bragaglia died in Rome on July 15, 1960.

Filmography

- *Thais* (1917)
- *Il mio cadavere* (1917)
- *Vele ammainate* (1931)
- *Perfido incanto* (1918)
- *Un dramma nell'Olimpo* (1917)

Notes and references

This article comes largely from Anton Giulio Bragaglia article on the Italian Wikipedia.

External links

- Anton Giulio Bragaglia [1] at the Internet Movie Database

David Burliuk

David Davidovich Burliuk (Ukrainian: Давид Давидович Бурлюк; Russian: Давид Давидович Бурлюк) (July 21, 1882 – January 15, 1967) was a Ukrainian avant-garde artist (Futurist, Neo-Primitivist), book illustrator, publicist, and author associated with Russian Futurism. In the words of his publisher Maria (also Maryussia) Burliuk, David Burliuk was the father of "Soviet Russian Futurism."

Biography

David Burliuk was born in Semyrotivka near the village of Riabushky (now Lebedyn District, Sumy Oblast) in Ukraine, brother of Volodymyr (Wladimir) Burliuk in a family descended from Ukrainian Cossacks who held premier positions in the Hetmanate. His mother, Ludmila Mikhnevich, was of ethnic Belarussian descent. Because of his given name of "David," Burliuk was frequently mistaken for a Jew.

From 1898 to 1904 he studied at the art schools in Kazan and in Odessa, as well as at the Royal Academy in Munich. His exuberant, extroverted character was recognized by Anton Azhbe, his professor at the Munich Academy, who called Burliuk a "wonderful wild steppe horse."

In 1908 an exhibition with the group *Zveno* ("The Link") in Kiev was organized by David Burliuk together with Wladimir Baranoff-Rossine, Alexander Bogomazov, Volodymyr (Wladimir) Burliuk and Aleksandra Ekster.

From 1910 he was the member of the group *Jack of Diamonds*.

From 1910 to 1911 he attended the Art School in Odessa. After 1911 David concetrated on poetry.

From 1911 to 1913 he studied at the Moscow School of Painting, Sculpture and Architecture (MUZHZV).

In 1911 Burliuk participated in the group exhibition of the Blaue Reiter in Munich, which also included his brother Wladimir.

In 1912 David Burliuk was co-author of the Russian Futurist manifesto *A Slap in the Face of Public Taste*.

In 1913 he was expelled from the Academy. In the same year D. Burliuk founded the publishing venture of the futuristic writer's group *Hylaea*.

In 1915 David Burliuk published the book *The Support of the Muses in Spring*, with illustrations by Lentulov, and by David and Wladimir Burliuk.

From 1915 to 1917 he resided in the Urals with frequent trips to Moscow and Petrograd (St. Petersburg).

In 1917 he participated in an exhibition with the group *Jack of Diamonds* in the artists' salon in Moscow, which included Aleksandra Ekster and Kazimir Malevich.

From 1918 to 1922 he travelled to the USA via Siberia, Japan, and Canada.

In 1925 Burliuk was a co-founder of the Association of Revolutionary Masters of Ukraine (ARMU) with the members Alexander Bogomazov, Vasiliy Yermilov, Vadym Meller, Alexander Khvostenko-Khvostov, and Palmov Victor.

In 1927 he participated in an exhibition of the Latest Artistic Trends in the Russian Museum in Leningrad (St. Petersburg), together with Kazimir Malevich, Aleksandr Shevchenko, and Vladimir Tatlin.

David Burliuk was author of autobiographical sketches *My Ancestors, Forty Years: 1890–1930.*

In 1909 Burliuk painted a portrait of his future wife, Marussia, on a background of flowers and rocks on the Crimean coast. Many times thereafter he would set the image of his wife to canvas. Without question two dreams possessed his heart all his life: the face of his wife and the portrait of his homeland - first Ukraine and then his adopted country, the United States.

In 1945 an exhibit was mounted at [Irving Plaza| Irving Place Theater] in [New York City]

In 1962 he and his wife travelled to Australia where he held an exhibition at Moreton Galleries, Brisbane. It was his only Australian exhibition. During his stay there David Burliuk painted some sketches and works with Australian views.

From 1937 to 1966 Burliuk and his wife, Marussia, published *Color & Rhyme*, a periodical primarily concerned with charting Burliuk's activities.

In 1940, Burliuk petitioned the Soviet government for a request to visit his homeland. In exchange, he offered a sizeable collection of archival material pertaining to his contemporary and friend Vladimir Mayakovsky, which Burliuk offered to donate to the Mayakovsky Museum in addition to over 100 original paintings. Burliuk's requests were denied. He was allowed to visit the Soviet Union only in 1956 and 1965.

David Burliuk died on Long Island, New York.

Trivia

- A painting (most likely - fictional) by Burliuk appears in the novel *Chapayev and Void* by Viktor Pelevin. The painting is described as a black writing though a stencil of the word GOD.

External links and references

- Exhibition **Futurism and After: David Burliuk, 1882-1967** The Ukrainian Museum in New York, USA. October 31, 2008 - April 26, 2009 [7]

- Exhibition **Crossroads: Modernism in Ukraine, 1910-1930**,(2006-2007) The Ukrainian Museum in New York, USA. [1]
- REVISITING THE PAST: David Burliuk, father of Ukrainian Futurism in America [2]
- David Burliuk [3] at 100 Soviet painters gallery [4]
- Figureworks.com/20th Century work [5] at www.figureworks.com
- English translations of 4 poems, 1910-1915 [6]

Wladimir Burliuk

Wladimir Burliuk (Ukrainian: **Володимир Давидович Бурлюк**, Russian: **Владимир Давидович Бурлюк**, 1886–1917) was an avant-garde artist (Neo-Primitivist and Cubo-Futurist), book illustrator.

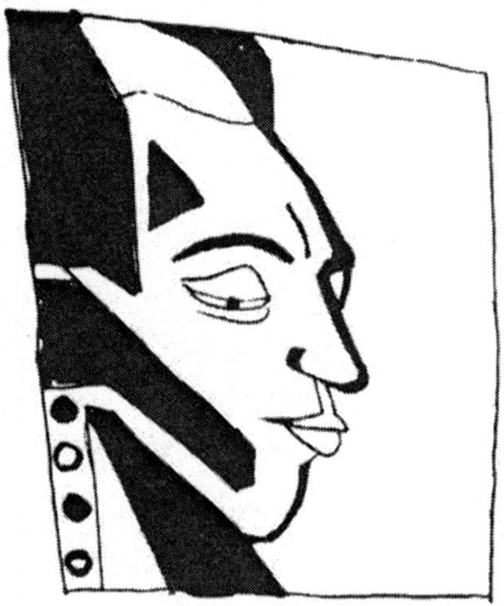

Wladimir Burliuk, Portrait of Velemir Khlebnikov, 1913

Biography

Burliuk was born on March 27, 1886 in Kharkiv, the brother of David Burliuk.

In 1903 he studied at Azbe School in Munich.

In 1904 he was a soldier in the Russo-Japanese War.

In 1905-1910 Burliuk attended the Kiev Art School (KKHU).

In 1907-1908 he lived in Moscow.

In 1908 he returned to Kiev and was in close contact with Aleksandra Ekster and Mikhail Larionov. Together with the members of the group *The Link (Zveno)* W. Burliuk and D. Burliuk organized an avant-garde exhibition in Kiev.

In 1909-1910 he lived in St.Petersburg and in 1910-1911 he lived in Moscow.

In 1910 he became the member of the group *Jack of Diamonds* together with D. Burliuk, Ekster, Malevich (later also Nathan Altman and Wladimir Tatlin). In the same year he became the member of the group of avant-garde artists known as the *Soyuz Molodyozhi (Union of the Youth).*

In 1911 he joined the art school in Odessa.

In 1913-1915 he illustrated many futuristic publications in Moscow, among them was the book *The Assistance of the Muses in Spring* (1915).

In 1916 he was drafted into military service.

In 1917 Wladimir Burliuk was killed in World War I in Saloniki.

References

- Wladimir Burliuk article ot Terra-Futura website [1] (Russian)

Mario Carli

Mario Carli (December 30, 1888 – September 9, 1935) was an Italian poet, novelist, essayist, diplomat, and journalist.

Life

Carli was born in San Severo, Apulia, to Florentine father and Apulian mother.

He spent his formative years in Florence, where he met Filippo Tommaso Marinetti in the 1910s, and adhered to Futurism as a member of the so-called *pattuglia azzurra* ("Azure platoon"). After fighting in World War I, he engaged in favor of the *Arditi*, and reached Gabriele D'Annunzio during the latter's political experiment in occupied Fiume in 1919. Carli then supported the militant anti-fascist *Arditi del Popolo*, created in 1920.

A successful journalist, Carli adhered to Benito Mussolini's Fascist movement the moment it started; he and his friend Emilio Settimelli published the intimidating newspaper *L'Impero*. Nonetheless, he proved to be a dissident, and joined the field of those considered "left-wing fascists". In the 1930s, Carli was Italy's consul general in Porto Alegre, Brazil.

Tormented by illness, he died prematurely in Rome.

Works

Carli wrote extensively, producing works like the experimental novel *Retroscena* ("Background"; 1915), and the memoir *Con d'Annunzio a Fiume* ("With D'Annunzio in Fiume"; 1920). In 1923 he published *La mia divinità* ("My Divinity"), a text in which he gathered his poetry, small poems in prose among which stands out *Notti filtrate* ("Filtered Nights") - a pre-Surrealist piece of importance.

The writings express Carli's conviction in life as energy, an egoistical effort at realising oneself against all odds and perils.

Carlo Carrà

Carlo Carrà	
Born	February 11, 1881 Quargnento, Italy
Died	April 13, 1966 (aged 85) Milan, Italy
Field	Painting
Movement	Futurist

Carlo Carrà (February 11, 1881 – April 13, 1966) was an Italian painter, a leading figure of the Futurist movement that flourished in Italy during the beginning of the 20th century. In addition to his many paintings, he wrote a number of books concerning art. He taught for many years in the city of Milan.

Biography

Carrà was born in Quargnento, near Alessandria (Piedmont). At the age of 12 he left home in order to work as a mural decorator.

In 1899-1900, Carrà was in Paris decorating pavilions at the Exposition Universelle, where he became acquainted with contemporary French art. He then spent a few months in London in contact with exiled Italian anarchists, and returned to Milan in 1901. In 1906, he enrolled at Brera Academy (*Accademia di Brera*) in the city, and studied under Cesare Tallone. In 1910 he signed, along with Umberto Boccioni, Luigi Russolo and Filippo Tommaso Marinetti the *Manifesto of Futurist Painters*, and began a phase of painting that became his most popular and influential.

Carrà's Futurist phase ended around the time World War I began. His work, while still using some Futurist concepts, began to deal more clearly with form and stillness, rather than motion and feeling. Carrà soon began creating still lifes in a style he, along with Giorgio de Chirico, called "metaphysical painting". Throughout the 1920s and 1930s, the metaphysical phase gave way to a sombre style akin to Masaccio's. An example from this period is his 1928 *Morning by the Sea*.

He is best known for his 1911 futurist work, *The Funeral of the Anarchist Galli*. Carrà was indeed an anarchist as a young man but, along with many other Futurists, later held more reactionary political views, becoming ultra-nationalist and irredentist before and during the war, as well as by Fascism after 1918 (in the 1930s, Carrà signed a manifesto in which called for support of the state ideology through art). The *Strapaese* group he joined, founded by Giorgio Morandi, was strongly influenced by fascism and responded to the neo-classical guidelines which had been set by the regime after 1937 (but was opposed to the ideological drive towards strong centralism).

He died in Milan in 1966.

Selected works

- *The Funeral of the Anarchist Galli* (1911)
- *The Enchanted Chamber* (1917)
- *The Metaphysical Muse* (1917)
- *The Daughter of the West* (1919)
- *The Engineer's Lover* (1921)

References

- Carrà at the Peggy Guggenheim Collection [1]
- Carrà at the Mart, Museo d'Arte Moderna e Contemporanea di Trento e Rovereto [2]
- Mark Antliff, "Fascism, Modernism, and Modernity", in *The Art Bulletin*, March 2002 [3]
- Karen Pinkus, *Bodily Regimes: Advertising under Italian Fascism*, Minneapolis-Saint Paul, University of Minnesota Press, 1995 ISBN 0816625638
- Stanislao G. Pugliese, *Italian Fascism and Anti-Fascism: A Critical Anthology*, Manchester, Manchester University Press, 2001 ISBN 071905639X

External links

- Ten Dreams Galleries [4]

Ambrogio Casati

Ambrogio Casati (December 27, 1897 – July 19, 1977) was an Italian painter.

He was born in Voghera, Italy in 1897 and was schooled in Paris in the plastic arts. Upon his return to Italy, he became associated with Filippo Tommaso Marinetti and the Futurist movement that was gaining force in the Italian arts scene of the time. His best-known pieces include *The Dance of the Chairs* (1931) and *Portrait of Marinetti* (1927). Casati was also the mentor of the future computer art pioneer Aldo Giorgini.

Casati died in Pavia in 1977.

Primo Conti

Primo Conti (October 16, 1900 —November 12, 1988) was an Italian Futurist artist.

Conti was born in Florence. Between the ages of 8 and 9, his precocious talent in the fields of music, poetry and painting was showing signs of his genius. In 1913 he met the Futurists.

His attraction to the latest innovations was expressed in almost completely Futurist forms in his drawings, while he developed a unique style in his painting that was a mixture of Art Nouveau, Fauvism, Expressionism and Orphism. It was not until 1917, after meeting with Giacomo Balla in Rome, and with Filippo Tommaso Marinetti in Naples (who later enthusiastically praised Conti's book *Imbottigliature* which was about to be printed) that Conti became part of the Futurist movement. His contribution to the movement was not only his literary works, but also the paintings and drawings he produced between 1917 and 1919 —the years in which his work was taking on the metaphysical trend.

The 1920s were a complex period for Conti. He explored Mannerism, Exoticism, Pittura Metafisica, and great historical and religious painting, covering a vast area that can be compared with his keen interest in the theatrical and literary world of Luigi Pirandello, Massimo Bontempelli and Enrico Pea, which led him to found the Viareggio Prize in 1929.

The 1930s brought a series of alternating events that created problems in his private life and led to his celebrative paintings. The decade also saw his enforced adhesion to Fascism (joining the Partito Nazionale Fascista), and his inner rebellion against it which transpired from his refusal to join Margherita Sarfatti's Novecento Italiano group and from other episodes when he stepped out of line. New prospects were only opened up to him when he became involved in designing stage sets for the opera house with the foundation of the Maggio Musicale Fiorentino.

By the 1940s, long before the official rediscovery (20 years later) of the Futurist movement, Conti was again working on Futurist subjects and experiments. From 1948 to 1963 he followed the rules of the Order of the Franciscans, though he still continued to paint.

Many of his works are housed in the Museo Primo Conti (Primo Conti Foundation Museum[1]) in the Villa le Coste at Fiesole (near Florence).

External links

- Official website of Fondazione Primo Conti [1]

Tullio Crali

Tullio Crali (Igalo, 1910 – Milan, 5 August 2000) was an Italian artist associated with Futurism. A self-taught painter, he was a late adherent to the movement, not joining until 1929. He is noted for realistic paintings that combine "speed, aerial mechanisation and the mechanics of aerial warfare", though in a long career he painted in other styles as well.

Crali was born in the Bay of Kotor on the coast of Montenegro. His family lived in Zadar until 1922, when they returned to Italy, living at Gorizia. At the age of fifteen, while a student at the local technical institute, Crali discovered Futurism. He took up painting, influenced by Giacomo Balla and Enrico Prampolini.

In 1928 Crali flew for the first time. His enthusiasm for flying and his experience as a pilot influenced his art. In 1929, through Sofronio Pocarini, he made contact with Marinetti, the founder of Futurism, and joined the movement. In the same year *aeropittura* was launched in the manifesto, *Perspectives of Flight*, signed by Benedetta, Depero, Dottori, Fillia, Marinetti, Prampolini, Somenzi and Tato. The manifesto stated that "The changing perspectives of flight constitute an absolutely new reality that has nothing in common with the reality traditionally constituted by a terrestrial perspective" and that "Painting from this new reality requires a profound contempt for detail and a need to synthesise and transfigure everything."

Despite his relative youth, Crali played a significant part in *aeropittura*. His earliest *aeropitture* represent military planes, *Aerial Squadron* and *Aerial Duel* (both 1929). In the 1930s, his paintings became realistic, intending to communicate the experience of flight to the viewer.. His best-known work, *Nose Dive on the City* (1939), shows an aerial dive from the pilot's point of view, the buildings below drawn in dizzying perspective.

Crali exhibited in Trieste and Padua. In 1932 Marinetti invited him to exhibit in Paris in the first *aeropittura* exhibition there. He participated in the Rome Quadrennial in 1935, 1939 and 1943 and the Venice Biennale of 1940. At that time Crali was researching signs and scenery, leading in 1933 to his participation in the film exhibition *Futuristi Scenotecnica* in Rome. In 1936 he exhibited with Dottori and Prampolini in the International Exhibition of Sports Art at the Berlin Olympics.

Crali's declamatory abilities and his friendship with Marinetti led him to organise Futurist evenings at Gorizia, Udine and Trieste, where he read the manifesto *Plastic Illusionism of War and Protecting the*

Earth which he had co-authored with Marinetti. He also published a *Manifesto of Musical Words - Alphabet in Freedom.*

Crali lived in Turin after the war, where he continued to promote Futurist events. Despite the ending of the Futurist movement with the death of Marinetti in 1944 and its Fascist reputation, Crali remained attached to its ideals and aesthetic.

Between 1950 and 1958 he lived in Paris, making occasional visits to Britain. He moved to Milan in 1958 where he remained (apart from a five-year period teaching at the Italian Academy of Fine Arts, Cairo) for the rest of his life. In Milan he began to collect and catalogue documents relating to his life and work. He donated his archive and several of his works to the Museo di arte moderna e contemporanea di Trento e Rovereto.

In 1959 he published the first post-war Futurist manifesto *Sassintesi* ("Stone Syntheses"). In it he advocated a new form of artistic expression using natural materials - pebbles, stones and rocks formed of various minerals. "The inherent qualities of colour, form, translucence, texture, etc. were to suggest, develop and determine the idea of the artist, while their appearance and positioning produced a harmonious composition that relied much on the stones' natural symbiosis with the cosmos." His *sassintesi* were exhibited in Milan in 1961. He tried to revive *aeropittura* in the late 1960s in a manifesto *Orbital Art*. His painting *Frecco Tricolori* (1966) depicts jet fighter planes. He continued to paint, sculpt, teach and lecture throughout the 'sixties, 'seventies and into the 'eighties.

At his own wish, Crali was buried at Macerata, which remains the home of his family.

References

- Italian Wikipedia entry on Crali
- Galleria d'arte moderna Udine biography of Crali [1]
- Osborn, B.,*Tullio Crali: The Ultimate Futurist Aeropainter* [2]
- Museo d'Arte Moderna e Contemporeana di Trento e Rovera [3]

Luigi De Giudici

Luigi de Giudici	
Selfportrait, 1910	
Birth name	Luigi De Giudici
Born	December 19, 1887 Pavia di Udine
Died	February 16, 1955 Venice
Nationality	Italian
Field	Painting
Movement	Futurism

Luigi De Giudici (December 12, 1887, Pavia di Udine – February 16, 1955) was an Italian painter. One of the protagonists of the Venetian anti-academic movement in the first twentieth century years. His works were exhibited at Ca' Pesaro in 1912-1920 and at Internation Exposition of Paris (1937).

Ca' Pesaro painter of Friuli origins in father's side and Carnia origin's on mother's side, he artistically grew up in Venice. Starting from the representation of a *living room world* of liberty taste, also through the irony of caricature, he was sensible to the avant-garde movements of the beginning of the twentieth century, from the Futurism to the Expressionism, from the movement of Pont-Aven to the Secessions in Wien and Munich. He artistically formed in the unrepeatable melting pot of styles and newness of the Barbantini's Ca' Pesaro of the 10es. Among his friends Boccioni, Gino Rossi, Arturo Martini, Mauroner, Pellis, Pomi.

In 1919, 32 years old, he decided to stop painting interrupting his carrier, almost hiding his paintings. He got married and had six children. He lived managing his prtopeties and was Major of Oderzo from 1925 to 1927. He went back to painting in 1931 for personal pleasure and finally stopped in 1937. When he died in Venice in 1955, his early paintings were found in a locked chest. Only by chance his son Angelo found his name in a list of exhibitors of Ca' Pesaro and in 1992 this interesting painter started to be studied.

Works

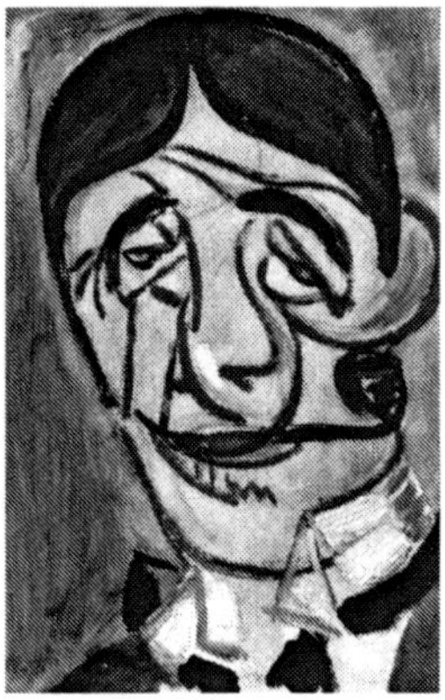

Uomo con pipa, 1916

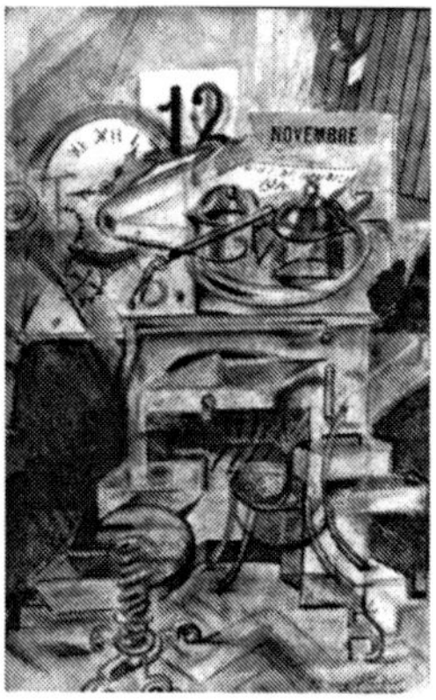

Il mio studio a Tolmezzo, 1916

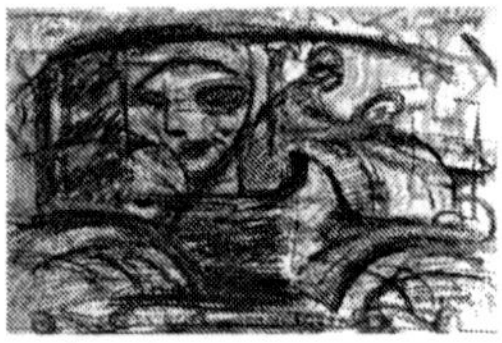

La bella sconosciuta, 1916

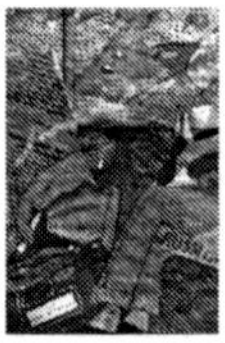

Viaggiare, 1916

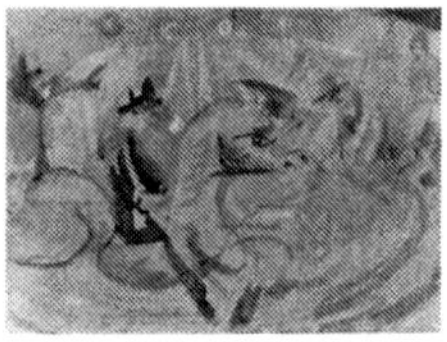

La giostra

Exhibitions

- **1912**
  - Venezia, Esposizione Permanente d'Arte e d'Industrie Veneziane, Ca' Pesaro, 29 June - 11 October
- **1913**
  - Venezia, Opera Bevilacqua La Masa - Esposizione Permanente d'Arte e d'Industrie Veneziane, Ca'Pesaro, 18 May - 5 October
- **1915**
  - Venezia, Esposizione di bozzetti degli artisti veneziani, Hotel Vittoria, 8–22 February
- **1919**
  - Milano, Grande Esposizione Nazionale Futurista, 'Galleria Centrale d'Arte', marzo, p. 10
  - Venezia, Esposizione d'Arte in Palazzo Pesaro, Ca' Pesaro, 15 July - 5 October
  - Lido di Venezia, Esposizione Nazionale di Belle Arti, 13 July

- Lido di Venezia, Mostra di bozzetti di pittura e scultura indetta dal Gruppo femminile dell'Associazione Trento - Trieste Sezione di Venezia, 17 August - 7 October
- Venezia, I^ Esposizione d'Arte del Circolo Artistico, Galleria Geri - Boralevi, 29 December - 2 February

- **1920**
  - Venezia, Esposizione Permanente d'Arti e d'Industrie veneziane, Ca' Pesaro, 17 July - 30 September
- **1921**
  - Treviso, Prima Mostra Regionale d'Arte, Palazzo Gabelli, September
  - Venezia, Esposizione del Circolo Artistico, July
- **1927**
  - Treviso, VII Mostra d'Arte Trevigiana, Salone dei 300, 16 October - 11 November
- **1936**
  - Venezia, XXVII Esposizione dell'Opera Bevilacqua La Masa VII del Sindacato Interprovinciale Fascista Belle Arti, Palazzo Reale, Sala Napoleonica, 15 April - 30 May
- **1937**
  - Venezia, XXVIII Esposizione dell'Opera Bevilacqua La Masa VIII del Sindacato Interprovinciale Fascista Belle Arti, Palazzo Reale, Sala Napoleonica, 15 April - 30 May
  - Parigi, Mostra d'Arte Italiana all'Esposizione Universale di Parigi
- **1999**
  - Venezia, Emblemi d'Arte da Boccioni a Tancredi. Cent'anni della Fondazione Bevilacqua La Masa 1899-1999, Galleria Bevilacqua La Masa, 6 March - 2 May
  - Modena, La Pittura a Venezia dagli anni di Ca' Pesaro alla Nuova Oggettività 1905-1940, Palazzo Montecuccoli, Fondazione della Cassa di Risparmio di Modena 28 November - 30 January
- **2000**
  - Venezia, Gigi De Giudici 1887 - 1955, Fondazione Querini Stampalia, 9 November - 10 dicember
- **2001**
  - Venezia, Donazione Eugenio Da Venezia, Fondazione Querini Stampalia, 10 November - 10 dicember
- **2002**
  - Oderzo, Gigi De Giudici e Oderzo, 1887-1955 Tra Futurismo e Novecento, Palazzo Foscolo, 26 April - 30 June
- **2004**

    - Mestre, Gigi De Giudici, 1887-1955 Tra modernità e tradizione, Centro Culturale Candiani, 29 January - 15 February
- **2005**
    - Tolmezzo, Luigi De Giudici Pittore Futurista in Carnia dal 1910 al 1920, Palazzo Frisacco, 30 July - 22 August
    - Spinea, De Giudici Olii e disegni, Oratorio di Santa Maria Assunta, 9–30 September
- **2007**
    - Torre di Mosto, Tra mare e laguna [1], Museo del paesaggio di Torre di Mosto, 16 June - 2 September
- **2008**
    - Torre di Mosto, La seduzione del paesaggio [2], Museo del paesaggio di Torre di Mosto, 12 July - 7 September

Further reading (in Italian)

- Gigi De Giudici 1887-1955 (catalogo della mostra, Fondazione Querini Stampalia), a cura di Giuseppina dal Canton, Venezia, Donazione Eugenio Da Venezia, quaderno n°7, Venezia, 9 Novembre-10 Dicembre2000
- Dizionario del Futurismo, a cura di E. Godoli, Ed. Vallecchi, Firenze, 2001, pp. 361–362
- Bromojodicherie tolmezzine 1914-17 ovvero....la gente di Tumiec durante la Grande Guerra nei disegni e caricature di Luigi De Giudici, di Pier Giuseppe Avanzato, Ed. Andrea Moro, Tolmezzo, 2005
- Dal "vero" accademico al naturalismo novecentista passando per l'avanguardia: le opere donate dagli Eredi De Giudici al Fondo Da Venezia , in Donazione Eugenio Da Venezia , Fondazione Scientifica Querini Stampalia, Venezia, 2001, pp. 79– 80 ("Quaderni della Donazione Eugenio Da Venezia", 8) Sito Università di Venezia [3]

External links

Further information: http://www.luigidegiudici.com [4]

Fortunato Depero

Fortunato Depero (March 30, 1892 - November 29, 1960) was an Italian futurist painter, writer, sculptor and graphic designer.

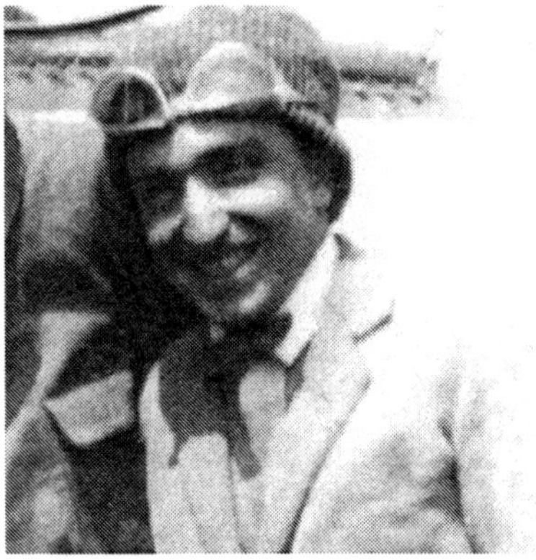

Fortunato Depero (1922)

Although born in Fondo (in the Italian Trentino region), Depero grew up in Rovereto and it was here he first began exhibiting his works, while serving as an apprentice to a marble worker. It was on a 1913 trip to Florence that he discovered a copy of the paper *Lacerba* and an article by one of the founders of the futurism movement, Filippo Tommaso Marinetti. Depero was inspired, and in 1914 moved to Rome and met fellow futurist Giacomo Balla. It was with Balla in 1915 that he wrote the manifesto *Ricostruzione futurista dell'universo* ("Futurist Reconstruction of the Universe") which expanded upon the ideas introduced by the other futurists. In the same year he was designing stage sets and costumes for a ballet.

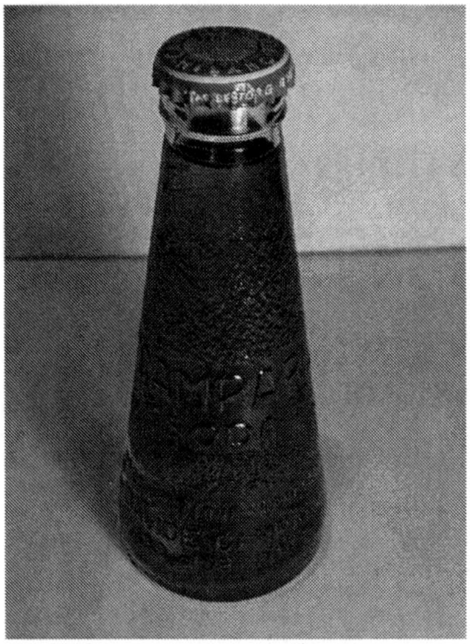

Depero's 1932 bottle design for Campari Soda is still in production

In 1919 Depero founded the "Casa d'Arte Futurista" (House of Futurist Art) in Rovereto, which specialised in producing toys, tapestries and furniture in the futurist style. In 1925 he represented the futurists at the Exposition Internationale des Arts Décoratifs et Industriels Modernes (International Exposition of Modern Industrial and Decorative Arts).

1928 saw Depero move to New York, where he experienced a degree of success, doing costumes for stage productions and designing covers for magazines including *Movie Maker*, *The New Yorker* and *Vogue*, among others. He also dabbled in interior design during his stay, working on two restaurants which were later demolished to make way for the Rockefeller Center. He also did work for the *New York Daily News* and Macy's, and built a house on West 23rd Street. In 1930 he returned to Italy.

In the 1930s and 40s Depero continued working, although due to futurism being linked with fascism, the movement started to wane. The artistic development of the movement in this period can mostly attributed to him and Balla. One of the projects he was involved in during this time was *Dinamo* magazine, which he founded and directed. After the end of the Second World War, Depero had trouble with authorities in Europe and in 1947 decided to try New York again. This time he found the reception not quite as welcoming. One of his achievements on his second stay in the United States was the publication of *So I Think, So I Paint*, a translation of his autobiography initially released in 1940: *Fortunato Depero nelle opere e nella vita* (literally, *Fortunato Depero, his works and his life*). From the winter of 1947 to late October 1949 Depero lived in a cottage in New Milford, Connecticut, relaxing and continuing with his long-standing plans to open a museum. His host was William Hillman, an associate of the then-President, Harry S. Truman.

After New Milford, Depero returned to Rovereto, where he would live out his days. In August 1959 Galleria Museo Depero opened, fulfilling one of his long-term ambitions. On November 29, 1960, after being ill with diabetes and spending the last two years unable to paint due to hemiparesis, Depero died age 68.

Many of his works are featured in the permanent collection of the Mart, the Museum of Modern and Contemporary Art of Trento and Rovereto [1]. The Casa d'Arte Futurista Depero, Italy's only museum dedicated to the Futurist movement, and containing 3,000 objects is now one of Mart's venues. Closed for many years for extensive refurbishment, the Casa d'Arte Futurista Depero has since re opened.

Writings

- *So I think, so I paint: Ideologies of an Italian self-made painter*, Mutilati e Invalidi, Trento, 1947 ASIN: B0007JG8YG

External links

- Official website in English, with biography and virtual museum [2]
- Fortunato Depero Art [3]

Nikolay Diulgheroff

Nikolay Diulgheroff (Bulgarian: Николай Дюлгеров, *Nikolay Dyulgerov*; 20 December 1901–9 June 1982) was a Bulgarian artist, designer and architect who was active in Italy as a prominent representative of interwar Italian Futurism (*il secondo Futurismo*).

Diulgheroff was born in Kyustendil, a town in the western part of the Principality of Bulgaria, to a printer father. In 1920 and 1921, he studied at the University of Applied Arts in Vienna, Austria. The following year he studied in Dresden, Germany, and in 1923 he enrolled at the original Bauhaus in Weimar, where he was close to Swiss expressionist Johannes Itten. While a student in Germany, Diulgheroff exhibited his art in Berlin and Dresden. In 1924, he had his separate exhibition in Sofia, the capital of Bulgaria.

In 1926, Diulgheroff settled in Turin, Italy, to study architecture at the Accademia Albertina, graduating in 1932. Bringing with him a characteristically Central European constructivist culture, he was introduced to many of the eminent Italian futurists, such as Fillià, and adopted that style. Diulgheroff created his most notable works in the 1920s and 1930s. Some of his art is exhibited in the Galleria Nazionale d'Arte Moderna in Rome. He contributed to the Futurist meals formulated in Filippo Tommaso Marinetti and Fillià's 1930 *Manifesto of Futurist Cooking*: the dish *pollofiat* was his idea and he co-designed the interior of the *Taverna Santopalato*, the prime establishment for futurist cuisine. He created posters for Cinzano and Amaro Cora and advertising for Campari. Diulgheroff was part of leading futurist exhibitions throughout the 1920s and 1930s, such as those in Turin, Leipzig, Paris, Florence, Barcelona, Mantua and Venice.

Diulgheroff died in Turin, the city where he spent 56 years, in 1982. Diulgheroff remained active as an artist almost until his death. He is an honorary citizen of Turin and art historian Enrico Crispolti considers him the greatest of all interwar artists.

Gerardo Dottori

Gerardo Dottori (Perugia, 11 November 1884 to 13 June 1977) was an Italian Futurist painter. He signed the *Futurist Manifesto of Aeropainting* in 1929. He was associated with the city of Perugia most of his life, living in Milan for six months as a student and in Rome from 1926-39.

Dottori's' principal output was the representation of landscapes and visions of Umbria, mostly viewed from a great height. Among the most famous of these is *Umbrian Spring* and *Fire in the City*, both from the early 1920s.

Life

Dottori was born in a working class family, losing his mother when he was eight years old.

He was admitted as a young man to the Academy of Fine Arts in Perugia, employed at the same time by an antique dealer. In 1906 he worked as a decorator in Milan, where he was able to visit museums and exhibitions. In 1907, after six months, he returned to Perugia because he could no longer find work. He resumed his studies in 1908, mixing in avant-garde art circles in Florence. In 1910 he began work with the magazine *Defense dell'Arte*.

In 1911 he went to Rome where he met Giacomo Balla and became an adherent of Futurism. In 1912 he joined the first Futurist group in Umbria. In 1915 he fought in the War, at the same time writing *parole in libertà* (words in freedom) which he published under the name G.Voglio.

In 1920 he founded the Futurist magazine *Griffa!* which took on the task of spreading Futurist ideas in Perugia. In the same year he had his first exhibition in Rome.

In 1924 he participated in the Futurist Congress, where he had already acquired a certain notoriety, presenting his thesis on *Rural Futurism*. In the same year he exhibited at the Venice Biennale, the first Futurist to do so, in the course of his life participating in ten Biennales.

From 1926 to 1939 he lived in Rome, contributing to various art magazines. In 1925 he exhibited at the Permanente and in 1927 at the Gallery Pesaro in the first of a series of Futurist exhibitions, including a one-man show in 1931.

His major contribution to Futurism was Aeropainting. He was one of the signatories of the 1929 *Aeropainting Manifesto*, signed also by Benedetta, Depero, Fillia, Marinetti, Prampolini, Somenzi and Tato (Guilielmo Sansoni), who are among its major representatives.

In 1932 he was one of the first Futurists to paint sacred subjects, following the *Futurist Manifesto of Sacred Art* (1931) signed by Marinetti and Fillia. The Futurist involvement in religious art followed the signing of the Lateran Treaty between the Vatican and Fascist Italy in 1929.

In 1939 Dottori was appointed to the chair of painting at Perugia, remaining in that post until 1947.

In 1941 he wrote the *Manifesto of Umbrian Aeropainting* in which he proposed that the essence of his Futurism lay in the representation of mystically-inclined landscapes.

Dottori carried out many mural commissions, including the Altro Mondo in Perugia and the hydroport in Ostia. Mural painting was embraced by the Futurists in the *Manifesto of Mural Plasticism* at a time when the revival of fresco painting was being debated in Italy.

Following a post-war silence around Marinetti's Futurism, Dottori exhibited in 1951 at Bergamini and the 1953 Biennale of Angelicum and continued to exhibit in the 1950s and 1960s. In 1989 a retrospective of Dottori's work was presented at the Gallery San Carlo.

Biographies

In 1966 a biography *Gerardo Dottori Futurist* was published by Vanni Scheiwiller and in 1968 Alberto Sartoris edited a small monograph. In 1970 the Milan magazine *Arts* devoted a special issue to Dottori and Guido Ballo wrote a monograph on him in the 1970. Franco Passoni, the Milanese critic, who had shown an early interest in aeropainting, has written about him since the early seventies.

References

- http://www.lattuadastudio.it/MostreArtecentro/dottori.htm
- Hulten, P., *Futurism and Futurisms*, Thames and Hudson, 1986
- Martin, S., *Futurism*, Taschen, n.d.

Fillià

Fillià (3 October 1904 – 10 February 1936) was the name adopted by **Luigi Colombo**, an Italian artist associated with the second generation of Futurism.

Fillià was born in Revello. He established the Futurist movement in Turin in 1923 at the age of 19 with a group which included Nikolay Diulgheroff, Pippo Oriani, Enrico Alimandi, Franco Costa and the sculptor Mino Rosso. Fillià quickly became the leader of the group and its principal theorist. He published the art reviews: *Futurismo* (*Futurism*) (1924), *Ventrina Futurista* (1927), *La Città Futurista* (*The Futurist City*) (1929), *La Città Nuova* (*The New City*) (1930-1934), and *Stile Futurista* (*Futurist Style*) (1934-1935) with Enrico Prampolini. His work in the mid-1920s shows the influence of Prampolini. After 1928, Fillià's work shows increasing subjectivity.

He became an exponent of *L'Aeropittura*, (Aeropainting), the dominant Futurist style of the 1930s which applied the experience of flight to the depiction of landscape aerially; the world was no longer seen from the perspective of the person on the ground but as if from an aeroplane. In 1929, he was a co-signatory of the Futurist manifesto *L'Aeropittura*, with Benedetta, Depero, Gerardo Dottori, Marinetti, Somenzi, Tato and Prampolini.

Fillià was the co-author with Marinetti of the *Manifesto of Futurist Cooking*, published in the Turin newspaper, *The People's Gazette* (*Gazetta del Popolo*), on 28 December 1930.

Enrico Crispolti says that Fillià and his colleagues in Turin explored an interior, psychological and subjective world, unlike other Futurists of the period such as Prampolini and Depero. Fillià had recourse to an "airy body," a "synthesis of movement, of the organic aspect, of the emotions of flight." The ectoplasmic forms which appear in Fillià's paintings of the late twenties and early thirties contrast with the rigidity of his earlier work and were taken up to explore the subconscious. His interest in the spiritual aspects of art turned to specifically religious painting from 1930 to 1933. He had large exhibitions at Padua (1931), La Spezia (1932) and Florence (1933) and in 1932 co-authored the *Manifesto of Sacred Futurist Art* with Marinetti.

He had an interest in architecture, designing the Futurist Pavilion at the 1928 International Exhibition in Turin.

Fillià's activities as an organizer and polemicist, which he continued through his contact with the avant-garde in his numerous trips to Paris, ended with his death at Turin in 1936 at the age of thirty-two.

There are works by Fillià in the collections of the Galleria d'Arte Moderna in Rome, the Galleria d'Arte Moderna in Turin, and in a number of private collections.

References

http://www.papillongallery.com/sold/Fillià

Filippo Tommaso Marinetti

Filippo Tommaso Marinetti	
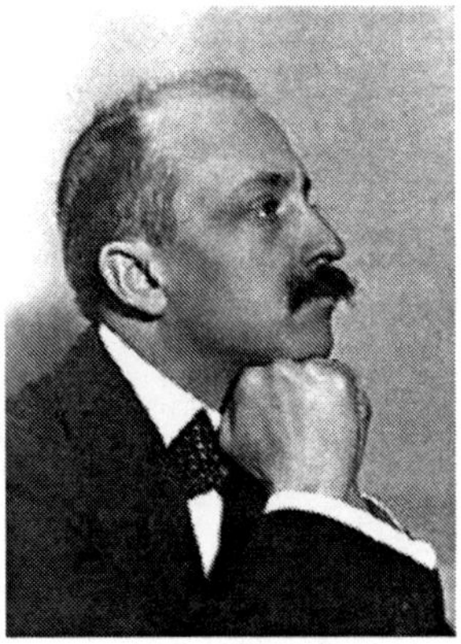	
Filippo Tommaso Marinetti	
Born	22 December 1876 Alexandria, Egypt
Died	2 December 1944 (aged 67) Bellagio, Italy
Occupation	Poet
Literary movement	Futurism

Filippo Tommaso Emilio Marinetti (December 22, 1876 – December 2, 1944) was an Italian ideologue, poet, editor, and founder of the Futurist movement.

Childhood and adolescence

Emilio Angelo Carlo Marinetti (some documents give his name as "Filippo Achille Emilio") spent the first years of his life in Alexandria, Egypt, where his father (Enrico M.) and his mother (Amalia Grolli) lived together *more uxorio* (as if married).

His love for literature emerged during his school years. At seventeen he started his first school magazine, *Papyrus*; the Jesuits threatened to expel him for bringing Emile Zola's scandalous novels to school.

He studied in Egypt and Paris, where he obtained the baccalaureat in 1893. He took a degree in law at Pavia University, graduating in 1899.

He decided never to be a lawyer but to follow his literary vocation. He experimented incessantly in every field of literature (poetry, narrative, theatre, *words in liberty*), signing everything "Filippo Tommaso Marinetti".

Futurism

Marinetti is widely known as the author of the Futurist Manifesto, which he wrote in 1908. It was published on the front page of the most prestigious French daily, Le Figaro, on February 20, 1909.

In *The Founding and Manifesto of Futurism*, Marinetti declared that "Art [...] can be nothing but violence, cruelty, and injustice." Since that text proclaims the unity of life and art, Marinetti understood violence not only as a means of producing an aesthetic effect, but also as being inherent to life itself. George Sorel, whose influence spanned the entire political spectrum from anarchism to Fascism, also argued for the importance of violence. Futurism had both anarchist and Fascist elements; Marinetti later became an active supporter of Benito Mussolini.

A great lover of speed, Marinetti had a minor car accident outside Milan in 1908 when he veered into a ditch to avoid two cyclists. He referred to the accident in the Futurist Manifesto: the Marinetti who was helped out of the ditch was a new man, determined to shake loose the pretense and decadence of the prevailing Liberty style. He outlined a new and strongly revolutionary programme to his friends, in which they should close off every bridge to the past, "destroy the museums, the libraries, every type of academy", and sing of "the great crowds, shaken by work, by pleasure or by rioting". Together, he wrote, "We will glorify war - the world's only hygiene - militarism, patriotism, the destructive gesture of freedom-bringers, beautiful ideas worth dying for, and scorn for woman."

The Futurist Manifesto was read and debated all across Europe, but Marinetti's first 'Futurist' works were not as successful. In April, the opening night of Le Roi Bombance (The Feasting King), written in 1905 was interrupted by loud, derisive whistling on the part of the audience... and by Marinetti himself, who thus introduced another essential element of Futurism, "the desire to be heckled." Marinetti did, however, fight a duel with a critic he considered too harsh.

Even his drama *La donna è mobile* (Poupées électriques), presented in Turin was not successful. Today, the play is remembered chiefly through a later version, titled *Elettricità sessuale* (Sexual Electricity), and chiefly for the appearance onstage of humanoid automatons, ten years before the Czech novelist Josef Čapek would invent the term "robot".

In 1910, his first novel *Mafarka il futurista* was cleared of all charges in an obscenity trial. That year, Marinetti discovered some allies in three young painters, (Umberto Boccioni, Carlo Carrà, Luigi Russolo), who joined the Futurist movement. Together with them (and with poets such as Aldo Palazzeschi), Marinetti launched a series of Futurist Evenings, theatrical spectacles in which the Futurists declaimed their manifestos in front of a crowd that, often as not, attended the performances in order to throw various vegetables at the Futurists.

The most successful "happening"' of that period was the launch of the Manifesto Against Past-Loving Venice from the belltower of Saint Mark's Basilica. In the flier, Marinetti calls for "fill(ing) the small, stinking canals with the rubble from the old, collapsing and leprous palaces" to "prepare for the birth of an industrial and militarized Venice, capable of dominating the great Adriatic, a great Italian lake."

In 1911, the Italo-Turkish War broke out and Marinetti did not shrink from the war-effort: he departed immediately for Libya as war correspondent for a French newspaper. His articles were eventually collected and published in *The Battle Of Tripoli*. He also made a number of visits to London, which he considered 'the Futurist city par excellence', and where a number of exhibitions, lectures and demonstrations of Futurist music were staged. However, although a number of artists, including Wyndham Lewis, were interested in the new movement, only one British convert was made, the young artist C.R.W. Nevinson. Nevertheless, Futurism was an important influence upon Lewis's Vorticist movement, which must be seen as its indirect offspring.

Around the same time he worked on a violently anti-Catholic and anti-Austrian verse-novel, *Le monoplan du Pape* (*The Pope's Aeroplane*, 1912) and edited an anthology of futurist poets. But his attempts to renew the language of poetry did not satisfy him. So much so that in his foreword to the anthology, he launched a new revolution: it was time to be done with traditional syntax and to move towards "words in freedom" (*parole in libertà*). His sound poem *Zang Tumb Tumb* exemplifies words in freedom. Recordings can be heard here of Marinetti reading some of his sound poems: *Battaglia, Peso + Odore* (1912) [1] *Dune, parole in libertà* (1914) [2] *La Battaglia di Adrianopoli* (1926) (recorded 1935) [3]

Marinetti and Fascism

In early 1918 he founded the *Partito Politico Futurista* or Futurist Political Party, which only a year later was absorbed into Benito Mussolini's *Fasci di combattimento*, making Marinetti one of the first supporters and members of the Italian Fascist Party. In 1919 he co-wrote with Alceste De Ambris the Fascist Manifesto, the original manifesto of the Italian Fascist movement. He opposed Fascism's later exaltation of existing institutions, calling them "reactionary," and, after walking out of the 1920 Fascist party congress in disgust, withdrew from politics for three years. However, he remained a notable force in developing the party thought throughout the regime's existence. For example, at the end of the *Congress of Fascist Culture* that was held in Bologna on March 30, 1925, Giovanni Gentile addressed Sergio Panunzio on the need to define Fascism more purposefully by way of Marinetti's opinion, stating, "Great spiritual movements make recourse to precision when their primitive inspirations - what F. T. Marinetti identified this morning as artistic, that is to say, the creative and truly innovative ideas, from which the movement derived its first and most potent impulse - have lost their force. We today find ourselves at the very beginning of a new life and we experience with joy this obscure need that fills our hearts - this need that is our inspiration, the genius that governs us and carries us with it." Thus Futurism continued to influence Fascist thinkers outside of the Futurist movement.

Throughout the Fascist regime Marinetti sought to make Futurism the official state art of Italy but failed to do so. Mussolini was personally uninterested in art and chose to give patronage to numerous styles and movements in order to keep artists loyal to the regime. Opening the exhibition of art by the Novecento Italiano group in 1923 he said, "I declare that it is far from my idea to encourage anything like a state art. Art belongs to the domain of the individual. The state has only one duty: not to undermine art, to provide humane conditions for artists, to encourage them from the artistic and national point of view." Mussolini's mistress, Margherita Sarfatti, who was as able a cultural entrepreneur as Marinetti, successfully promoted the rival Novecento Group, and even persuaded Marinetti to sit on its board.

Although in the early years of Italian Fascism, modern art was tolerated and even embraced, towards the end of the 1930s, right-wing Fascists introduced the concept of "degenerate art" from Germany to Italy and condemned Futurism. In 1938, hearing that Adolf Hitler wanted to include Futurism in a traveling exhibition of degenerate art, Marinetti persuaded Mussolini to refuse to let it enter Italy. In the same year he protested publicly against anti-Semitism.

Marinetti made numerous moves to ingratiate himself with the regime, becoming less radical and avant garde with each. He moved from Milan to Rome to be nearer the centre of things. He became an academician despite his condemnation of academies, saying, “It is important that Futurism be represented in the Academy.” He married despite his condemnation of marriage, promoted religious art after the Lateran Treaty of 1929 and even reconciled himself to the Catholic church, declaring that Jesus was a Futurist.

There were other contradictions in his character: despite his nationalism, he was an international figure, educated in Egypt and France, writing his first poems in French, publishing the Futurist Manifesto in a French newspaper and tirelessly traveling to promote his movement.

Marinetti volunteered for active service in the Second Italo-Abyssinian War and the Second World War, serving on the Eastern Front, despite his advanced age.

He died of cardiac arrest while working on a collection of poems praising the wartime achievements of the Decima Flottiglia MAS in Bellagio, Italy on December 2, 1944.

External links

- ItalianFuturism.org: news, exhibitions, and scholarship pertaining to the Futurist Movement [8]
- Works by Filippo Tommaso Marinetti [4] at Project Gutenberg
- Image of Le Figaro with *Le Futurisme* (1909) [5]
- Score to the sound poem *Dune, parole in libertà* (1914) [6]
- Marinetti's "La Battaglia di Adrianopoli" (1926) recorded by Marinetti in 1935 [7] published at Tellus Audio Cassette Magazine
- Marinettis' the Futurist Sensibility [8]
- Zang Tumb Tumb [9]
- Filippo Tommaso Marinetti Papers [10] Photographs, postcards, and writings from the Beinecke Rare Book and Manuscript Library at Yale University [11]
- Filippo Tommaso Marinetti's Libroni on Futurism [12] Images derived from slides taken of seven scrapbooks compiled by Marinetti between 1905 and 1944 from the Beinecke Rare Book and Manuscript Library at Yale University [11]
- Marinetti student notebooks and other papers, 1891-1936. Research Library at the Getty Research Institute. Los Angeles, California. [13] The collection includes class notes, essays and stories that Marinetti wrote for secondary school in Alexandria, Egypt. One notebook was written by Leone Marinetti. There is also correspondence, 1891–1936, a small amount of which is with school friends and the school rector, but most of which concerns the futurist enterprise. There are letters from Gino Severini, Gabriele D'Annunzio, Umberto Boccioni, Mario Carli, Benedetto Croce, B. Bottai, Giovanni Pascoli, and Paolo Orano, among others, and from Marinetti's French publisher Sansot. There is a small number of Marinetti's writings, primarily dramas and "syntheses," generally in typescript.
- Marinetti correspondence and papers, 1886-1974. Research Library at the Getty Research Institute. Los Angeles, California. [14] Arranged in eight series: Series I. Letters and submissions to Marinetti and others, 1900–1974; Series II. Unsigned or undated letters and submissions, ca. 1910-ca. 1970; Series III. Letters from Marinetti, ca. 1905-1944; Series IV. Writings by Marinetti, 1896–1949; Series V. Biographies, 1927–1968; Series VI. Photographs, 1886–1972; Series VII. Agenzia Letteraria Artistica (A.L.A.): Circulars, 1934–1939; Series VIII. Letters to Alberto Cappa, 1923-1931.
- Papers of F.T. Marinetti and Benedetta Cappa Marinetti, 1902-1965 (bulk 1920-1939). Research Library at the Getty Research Institute. Los Angeles, California. [15] Collection offers a view of F.T. Marinetti in the ceremonial role he played during Futurism's second phase. Includes minor manifesto manuscripts, generally typewritten, sometimes translated or excerpted; a number of minor literary manuscripts; and 20,000 slides that reproduce the contents of Marinetti's five scrapbooks. Material on Benedetta includes handwritten corrected drafts of her three novels, and a number of essays and speeches on women and art, women and Fascism, Futurism, and Marinetti. Some correspondence suggests the central role that Marinetti and Benedetta played relative to the other

Futurists, whose activities the collection selectively documents via manuscripts, photos, clippings, slides, posters, scrapbooks, and musical scores.

Angiolo Mazzoni

Angiolo Mazzoni (1894–1979) was one of the most brilliant and prolific Italian architects of the 1920s and 1930s. Mazzoni designed many public buildings during the 1920s and 1930s, among which post offices and train stations. He joined Futurism in the 1930s and co-authored the *Manifesto of Aerial Architecture* (signed also by F.T. Marinetti).

Stylistically rooted in nineteenth-century eclecticism, he was never formally associated with any of the Italian modern movement groups. He had however powerful links to "*seconda maniera*" (the second wave) Futurism, with connections to the Viennese School of Hoffman and Wagner, and a deeply rooted classical instinct. Throughout his work, his stylistic approach vacillated dramatically, from the overtly bombastic and classical to the dynamically modern. In every case, his handling of composition, solids and voids, light and shade, surfaces and materials, was originally conceived, spirited, poetic, erudite, strong, and full of conviction. After many years of neglect by architectural critics, his legacy is re-emerging and he is being acknowledged as one of the most outstanding Italian architects of the modern period.

Mazzoni was an able political mover, and married the daughter of Mussolini's Minister of Communications, Galeazzo Ciano; he owed much of his great success and influence to his intimate connections with the Fascist regime. He played a decisive role in using architecture to consolidate a positive image of Fascism throughout Italy, as chief architect for the Ministry of Communications and for the State Railways—two key modernizing sectors of the Fascist rebuilding programs.

Trento's Railway Station

A classic example of Mazzoni's work is the railway station in Trento, a city in the north-eastern Italian Alps, built during 1934–36. Trento had a special significance for the Fascist regime as the capital of the Trentino-Alto Adige (Welschtirol-Südtirol) region, annexed to Italy from Austria at the Treaty of Versailles after World War I. Mazzoni was born close to Trento.

The Fascist regime engaged in a comprehensive program of public works, during the years 1920–1940, leading to the construction of many new public buildings, and Mazzoni was the architect of many of them.

Trento's railway station represents Mazzoni's interpretation of the functionalist style typical of the times; the building's continuous windows and dynamic structural lines also express the Futurist idea of speed and streamlining. The station stands out due to its innovative use of advanced building materials, including steel and glass and the use of several varieties of local stone.

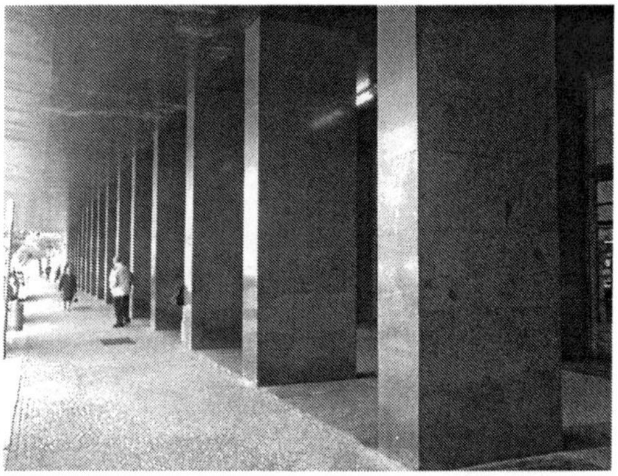

Trento station, front colonnade

The station offers platforms on four rail tracks and its design is intended to facilitate the flow of people from the street to the trains. Wide wood-frame doors open on the entire facade. A wide, shallow staircase leads to the underpassage to the 2nd and 3rd tracks. Spacious waiting space is provided under cover or indoor.

In addition to ticket offices, a tobacconist, a news-stand and baggage store, the station also provided office space for administration, restrooms, a restaurant and bar (today only a bar remains) and conference rooms and meeting space. Mazzoni was more than an architect. He also was an important interior and furniture designer, and all the components of his buildings, from wall decorations to brass door-handles and glazed screens, were designed by his office. The main hall of Trento railway station was decorated with large mosaics depicting the life of the people, and the natural beauties of the mountainous region around Trento. These depictions were typical of the time and served an educational-propagandistic purpose. Originally, the ceiling is said to have been painted light green.

Mazzoni's Legacy

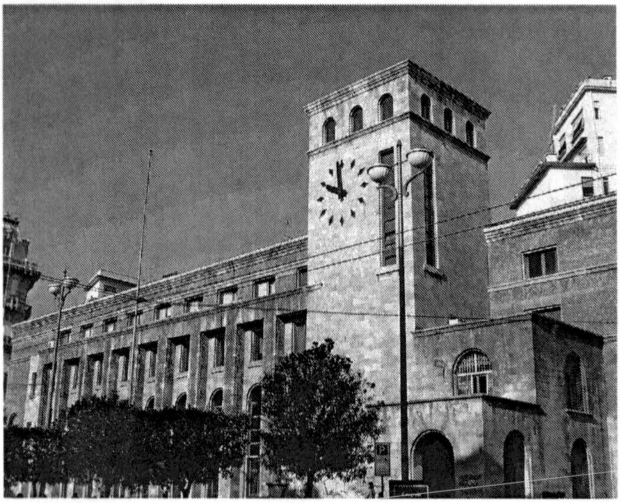

Central Post Office, La Spezia

All over Italy there are literally hundreds, if not thousands of large and small railway and telecommunications buildings by Mazzoni, still extant and functioning - a tribute to his mastery of robust, hard-working construction. That said, his relationship with Fascism has made it difficult for present-day Italian architecture culture to fully acknowledge his importance, and as a result many very important buildings by Mazzoni have been crudely altered or demolished in the post-war period. His own persisting Fascism, even after the end of the Second World War (when he left Italy for South America) did him no favors.

Of those buildings that still stand, a few are worth mentioning:

- the boiler house, control cabin and personnel facilities at Florence railway station (1934);
- the railway station of Siena (1933–35);
- the railway station at Montecatini Terme (1933–37).
- Roma Termini railway station, circa 1940

Recently, important academics and scholars (Ezio Godoli, Giorgio Muratore, Enrico Crispolti and others) have begun a rehabilitation process and a critical re-evaluation of Mazzoni. His archive is now kept at the Museum of Modern Art in Trento, and efforts are being made to ensure the conservation of his most important surviving buildings.

References

- *Angiolo Mazzoni (1894–1979)- Architetto Ingegnere del Ministero delle Communicazioni*, Milan, Skira, 2003. ISBN 88-8491-465-5
- Naomi Miller, Review of *Angiolo Mazzoni (1894–1979) - Architetto nell' Italia tra le due guerre*, in *The Journal of the Society of Architectural Historians*, Vol. 45, No. 1, (Mar., 1986), pp. 74–76

External links

- More information on Angiolo Mazzoni [1]
- Manifesto of Aerial Architecture [2]

Aldo Palazzeschi

Aldo Giurlani-Palazzeschi	
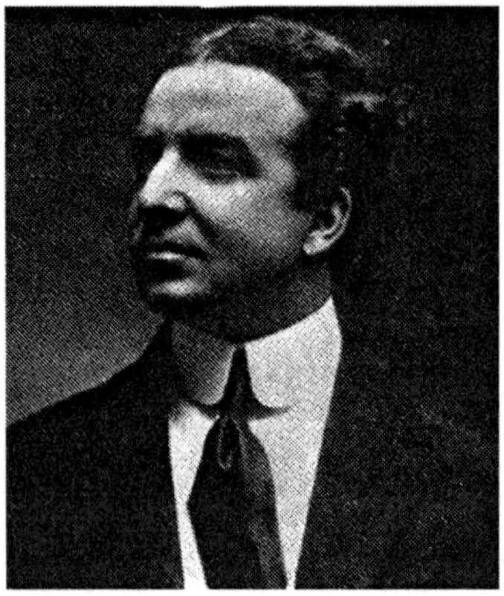	
Born	29 May 1885 Florence, Italy[1]
Died	17 August 1974 (aged 89) Rome, Italy
Occupation	Poet, Novelist, Journalist, Essayist
Literary movement	Neoavanguardia

Aldo Palazzeschi (2 February 1885 - 17 August 1974) was the pen name of **Aldo Giurlani**, an Italian novelist, poet, journalist and essayist.

Biography

He was born in Florence to a well-off, bourgeois family in Florence, and studied accounting and acting before he published his first book of poetry, *I cavalli bianchi* (in English, *The White Horses*) in 1905 using his maternal grandmother's name as a pseudonym. After meeting Filippo Tommaso Marinetti, he became a fervent Futurist. However, he was never entirely ideologically aligned with the movement and had a falling out with the group over Italy's involvement in World War I, which he opposed. His "futurist period" (roughly the 1910s) was a very fecund time in which he published a series of works that cemented his reputation. Most notable of these is his novel *Il codice di Perelà* (translated into English as *Man of Smoke*) published in 1911.

During the interwar era, his productivity lessened, as he became involved in journalism and other pursuits. Also during this time, he was a notable anti-Fascist. He returned with a series of novels in the late sixties and early seventies that resecured his place in the new, post-war avant-garde. He died in 1974 in his apartment in Rome. Today he is often considered an important influence on later Italian writers, especially those of the *neoavanguardia* in both prose and verse. His work is well noted by its "grotesque and fantastic elements"

Bibliography

- *I cavalli bianchi* (1905)
- *Lanterna* (1907)
- *Poemi* (1909)
- *L'incendiario* (1910)
- *Il codice di Perelà* (1911)
- *Il controdolore* (1914)
- *Due imperi... mancati* (1920)
- *L'interrogatorio della contessa Maria* (1925)
- *La piramide* (1926)
- *Stampe dell'Ottocento* (1932)
- *Sorelle Materassi* (1934)
- *Il palio dei buffi* (1936)
- *Allegoria di novembre* (1943)
- *Difetti 1905* (1947)
- *I fratelli Cuccoli* (1948)
- *Bestie del '900* (1951)
- *Roma* (1953)
- *Scherzi di gioventù* (1956)
- *Il buffo integrale* (1966)
- *Il doge* (1967)
- *Cuor mio* (1968)
- *Stefanino* (1969)
- *Storia di un'amicizia* (1971)
- *Via delle cento stelle* (1972)

External links

- [1] (In Italian)
- [2] (In Italian)
- Man of Smoke by Aldo Palazzeschi [3]

Giovanni Papini

Giovanni Papini	
Born	January 9, 1881 Florence
Died	July 8, 1956 (aged 75) Florence
Occupation	essayist, journalist, literary critic, poet, novelist
Nationality	Italian
Period	1903–1956
Genres	prose poetry, fantasy, autobiography, travel literature, satire
Subjects	political philosophy, history of religion
Literary movement	Futurism Modernism

Giovanni Papini (January 9, 1881 - July 8, 1956) was an Italian journalist, essayist, literary critic, poet, and novelist.

Early life

Born in Florence as the son of a modest furniture retailer (and former member of Giuseppe Garibaldi's Redshirts) from Borgo degli Albizi, Papini was baptized secretly to avoid the aggressive atheism of his father, and he lived a rustic, lonesome, and precociously introspective childhood. From that time onwards he felt a strong aversion to all beliefs, to all churches, as well as to any form of servitude (which he saw as connected to religion); he also became enchanted with the impossible idea of writing an encyclopedia wherein all cultures would be summarized.

Trained as a schoolteacher, he taught for a few years after 1899, then became a librarian. The literary life attracted Papini, who founded the magazine *Il Leonardo*, together with Giuseppe Prezzolini, in 1903, then joined Enrico Corradini's group as co-editor of *Il Regno*. He started publishing short-stories and essays: in 1903, *Il tragico quotidiano* ("The Tragic Everyday"), in 1907 *Il pilota cieco* ("The Blind Pilot") and *Il crepuscolo dei filosofi* ("The Twilight of the Philosophers"). The latter constituted a polemic with established and diverse intellectual figures, such as Immanuel Kant, Georg Wilhelm Friedrich Hegel, Auguste Comte, Herbert Spencer, Arthur Schopenhauer, and Friedrich Nietzsche - Papini proclaimed to the death of philosophers and the demolition of thinking itself. He briefly flirted with Futurism and other violent and liberating forms of Modernism (Papini is the character in several poems of the period written by Mina Loy).

Before and during World War I

After leaving *Il Leonardo* in 1907, Giovanni Papini founded *Anima* together with Giovanni Amendola. His *Parole e sangue* ("Words and Blood") essay of the period showed his unequivocal atheism, summoned in his advice:

> *Humans: become atheists each and all!... God will nevertheless welcome you with all [H]is heart!*

Furthermore, Papini sought to create scandal by speculating that Jesus and John the Apostle had a homosexual relationship.

He broke off with Prezzolini, co-editor of *Anima*, and the paper ceased to appear. Papini founded *Lacerba*, published between 1913 and 1915 (right before Italy's entry into World War I). In 1912, he published his best-known work, the autobiography *Un uomo finito* (tr.: "The Failure").

His 1915 collection of prose poetry *Cento pagine di poesia*, followed by *Buffonate* and *Maschilità*, and the 1916 *Stroncature* - Papini faced Giovanni Boccaccio, William Shakespeare, Johann Wolfgang von Goethe, but also contemporaries such as Benedetto Croce and Giovanni Gentile, and less prominent disciples of Gabriele D'Annunzio. He published verse in 1917, grouped under the title *Opera prima*. In 1921, Papini announced his newly-found Roman Catholicism, publishing the international bestseller essay *Storia di Cristo* ("Life of Christ").

Fascism and later years

After further verse works, he published the satire *Gog* (1931) and the essay *Dante vivo* (tr. "If Dante Were Alive"; 1933).

He moved towards Fascism, and his beliefs earned him a teaching position at the University of Bologna in 1935 (although his studies only qualified him for primary school teaching); the Fascist authorities confirmed Papini's "*impeccable reputation*" through the appointment. In 1937, Papini published the only volume of his *History of Italian Literature*, which he dedicated to Benito Mussolini: "*to Il Duce, friend of poetry and of the poets*", being awarded top positions in academia, especially in the study of Italian Renaissance. An Antisemite, he believed in an international plot of Jews, applauding the racial discrimination laws enforced by Mussolini in 1938.[*citation needed*] When the Fascist regime crumbled (1943), Papini entered the Franciscan convent in La Verna.

Largely discredited at the end of World War II, he was defended by the Catholic political right. His work concentrated on different subjects, including a biography of Michelangelo, while he continued to publish dark and tragic essays. He collaborated with *Corriere della Sera*, contributing articles that were published as a volume after his death.

According to *The Spectator*, NATO allegedly encouraged Papini, in 1951, to publish a fake interview with Pablo Picasso, to dramatically undercut his pro-Communist image. In 1962, the artist asked his biographer Pierre Daix, to expose the fake interview, which he did in *Les Lettres Françaises*.

References

- Biography partially taken from the introduction to *Gog* by Ettore Allodoli

External links

- Article on Papini at *Books and Writers* [1]
- Article on Papini at *Britannica Online* [2]
- A website about Giovanni Papini in Italian [3]
- A list of Papini's books translated in English [4]
- "Un uomo finito": website for the theater play about Giovanni Papini and John Henry Newman (in italian) [5]

Luigi Russolo

Luigi Russolo	
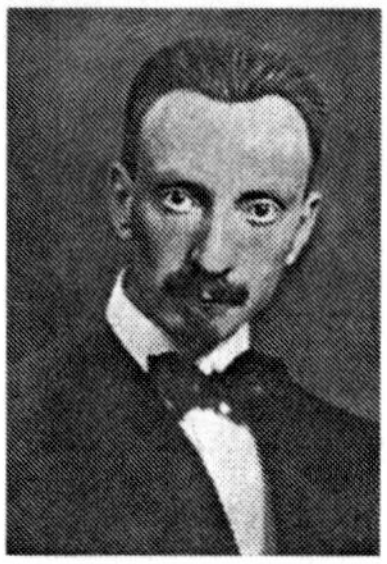 Luigi Russolo ca. 1916	
Background information	
Birth name	Luigi Russolo
Born	30 April 1883
Died	4 February 1947 (aged 63)
Genres	Experimental music
Occupations	"Machine music" pioneer Futurist painter Custom instrument builder
Years active	1901-1947

Luigi Russolo (30 April 1885 – 4 February 1947) was an Italian Futurist painter and composer, and the author of the manifesto *The Art of Noises* (1913). He is often regarded as one of the first noise music experimental composers with his performances of "noise concerts" in 1913-14 and then again after World War I, notably in Paris in 1921. He is also one of the first theorists of electronic music.

Biography

Luigi Russolo was perhaps the first noise artist. His 1913 manifesto, *L'Arte dei Rumori*, translated as *The Art of Noises*, stated that the industrial revolution had given modern men a greater capacity to appreciate more complex sounds. Russolo found traditional melodic music confining and envisioned noise music as its future replacement.

The *Art of Noises* classified "noise-sound" into six groups:

1. Roars, Thunderings, Explosions, Hissing roars, Bangs, Booms
2. Whistling, Hissing, Puffing

3. Whispers, Murmurs, Mumbling, Muttering, Gurgling
4. Screeching, Creaking, Rustling, Humming, Crackling, Rubbing
5. Noises obtained by beating on metals, woods, skins, stones, pottery, etc.
6. Voices of animals and people, Shouts, Screams, Shrieks, Wails, Hoots, Howls, Death rattles, Sobs

He designed and constructed a number of noise-generating devices called Intonarumori and assembled a noise orchestra to perform with them. A performance of his *Gran Concerto Futuristico* (1917) was met with strong disapproval and violence from the audience, as Russolo himself had predicted. None of his intoning devices have survived, though recently some have been reconstructed and used in performances. Although Russolo's works bear little resemblance to modern noise music, his pioneering creations cannot be overlooked as an essential stage in the evolution of this genre, and many artists are now familiar with his manifesto.

> At first the art of music sought purity, limpidity and sweetness of sound. Then different sounds were amalgamated, care being taken, however, to caress the ear with gentle harmonies. Today music, as it becomes continually more complicated, strives to amalgamate the most dissonant, strange and harsh sounds. In this way we come ever closer to *noise-sound.*

Antonio Russolo, another Italian Futurist composer and Luigi's brother, produced a recording of two works featuring the original Intonarumori. The 1921 made phonograph with works entitled *Corale* and *Serenata*, combined conventional orchestral music set against the famous noise machines and is the only surviving sound recording.

Russolo and Marinetti gave the first concert of Futurist music, complete with *intonarumori*, in April 1914 (causing a riot). The program comprised four "networks of noises" with the following titles:

- *Awakening of Capital.*
- *Meeting of cars and aeroplanes*
- *Dining on the terrace of the Casino* and
- *Skirmish in the oasis.*

All of his instruments were destroyed in World War II during the bombings on Paris. In 2009 replica's are being made for the Performa Festival in New York City, where his musical pieces were played.

See also

- Musica Futurista
- Experimental music
- Custom-made instruments
- List of custom-made instrument builders
- Noise music
- Futurism
- List of noise musicians

Further Reading & Audio Clips

Further reading

- Luigi Russolo's "The Art of Noises" [1]

Audio

- [2] mp3 audio files of the music of Luigi Russolo on UbuWeb
- Three audio clips by Luigi Russolo: *Serenata*, *Corale* and *Risveglio di una città*. (Thereminvox.com) [3]
- Modern recordings of noise intoners and a fragment of Luigi Russolo's key Futurist

References

Ian Chilvers & John Glaves-Smith, *A Dictionary of Modern and Contemporary Art*. Oxford University Press

External links

- *Intonarumori*: history, working and photographs of Russolo's Intonarumori (noise makers) at thereminvox.com [4]
- Media Art Net | Russolo, Luigi: Intonarumori (at medienkunstnetz.de) [5]
- Peggy Guggenheim Collection: Luigi Russolo [6]
- "Art of Noise" at zakros.com [7]
- JahSonic.com: Luigi Russolo [8]
- Bob Osborn's Futurism: Luigi Russolo [9]
- Prof. Russolo & His Noise Intoners [10]
- [2] mp3 audio files of the noise music of Luigi Russolo on UbuWeb
- Russolo's Intonarumori [11]

Valentine de Saint-Point

The French artist **Valentine de Saint Point** was one of the few women who worked with the Futurist movement. Her manifesto, "A Futurist Manifesto of Lust", dealt with the place of women within fascist ideology. She became a convert to Islam.

References

- *Tate Etc.* Summer 2009 (issue 16). Essay by Adrien Sina and Sarah Wilson. "Action feminine".

External links

- (French) Valentine de Saint Point, la Métachorie [1]

Antonio Sant'Elia

Antonio Sant'Elia (April 30, 1888 - October 10, 1916) was an extremely influential Italian architect.

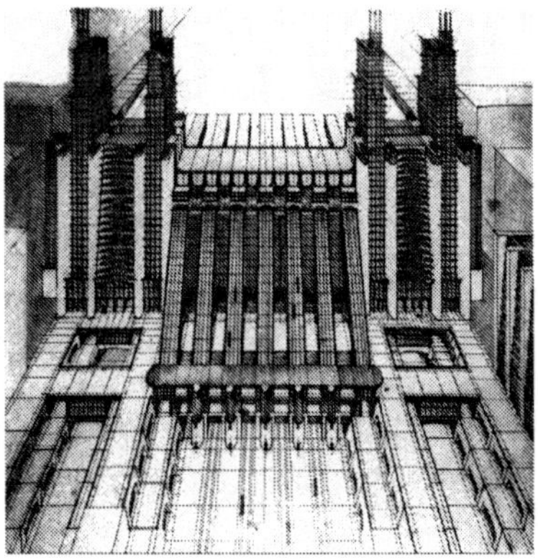

Perspective drawing from *La Citta Nuova*, 1914.

Life

Antonio Sant'Elia was born in Como, Lombardy. A builder by training, he opened a design office in Milan in 1912 and became involved with the Futurist movement. Between 1912 and 1914, influenced by industrial cities of the United States and the Viennese architects Otto Wagner and Adolf Loos, he began a series of design drawings for a futurist *Città Nuova* ("New City") that was conceived as symbolic of a new age.

Many of these drawings were displayed at the only exhibition of the *Nuove Tendenze* group (of which he was a member) exhibition in May/June 1914 at the "Famiglia Artistica" gallery. Today, some of these drawings are on permanent display at Como's art gallery (Pinacoteca). (They used to be in the Villa Olmo)

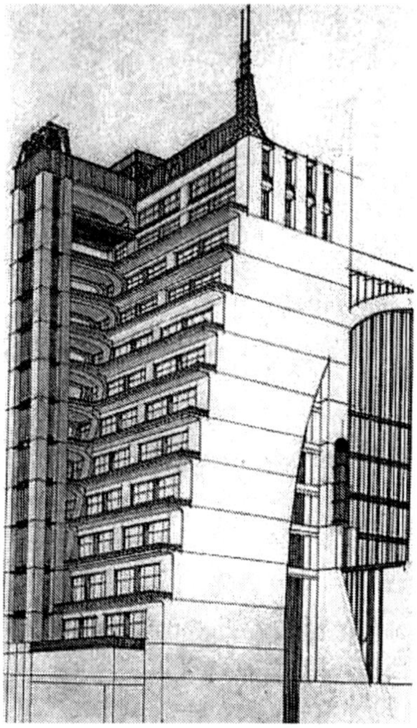

A perspective drawing by Sant'Elia, 1914

The manifesto *Futurist Architecture* was published in August 1914, supposedly by Sant'Elia, though this is subject to debate. In it the author stated that "*the decorative value of Futurist architecture depends solely on the use and original arrangement of raw or bare or violently colored materials*"[citation needed]. As described in this manifesto, his designs featured bold groupings and large-scale disposition of planes and masses creating a heroic industrial expressionism. His vision was for a highly industrialised and mechanized city of the future, which he saw not as a mass of individual buildings but a vast, multi-level, interconnected and integrated urban conurbation designed around the "*life*" of the city. His extremely influential designs featured vast monolithic skyscraper buildings with terraces, bridges and aerial walkways that embodied the sheer excitement of modern architecture and technology.

A nationalist as well as an irredentist, Sant'Elia joined the Italian army as Italy entered World War I in 1915. He was killed during the Battles of the Isonzo, near Monfalcone. Most of his designs were never built, but his futurist vision has influenced many architects, artists and designers.

Works

La Citta Nuova, 1914

See also

Futurist architecture

External links

- Website in Italian [1]
- Manifesto of Futurist Architecture [2]

Image gallery

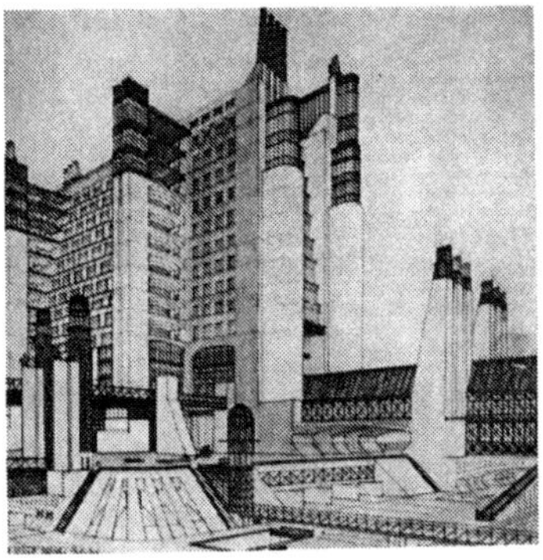

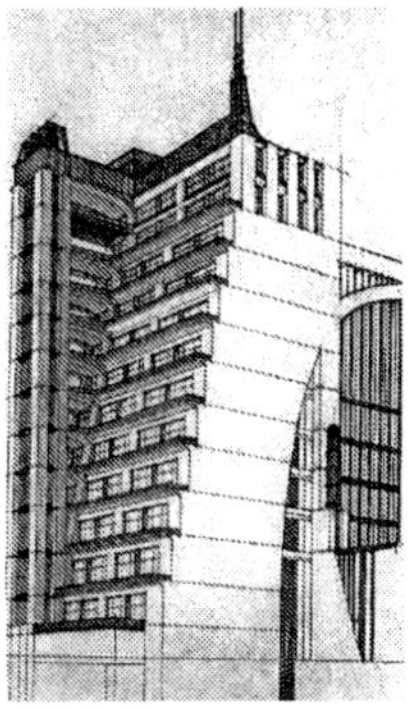

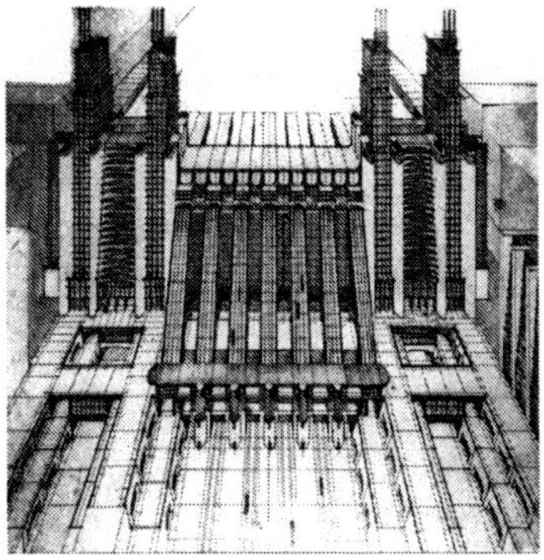

Jules Schmalzigaug

Jules Schmalzigaug (Antwerp, 1882 or 1883 (the sources have different data) - The Hague, May 13, 1917) was a Belgian futurist painter.

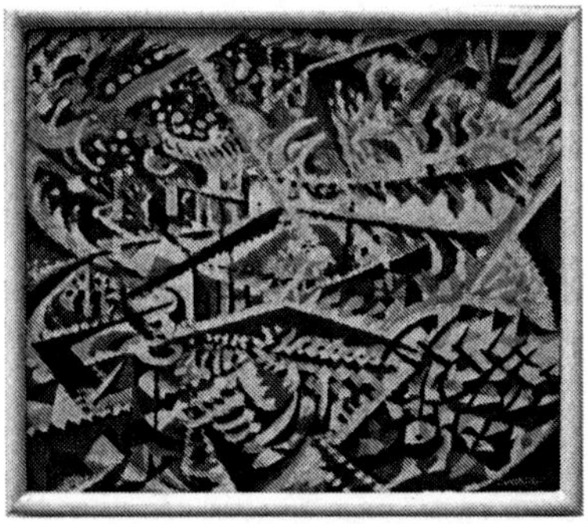

Impressions in a Dance Hall

His Life and Art

His well-to-do family came from Germany and lived in Antwerp. Schmalzigaug travelled a lot form his age of 16. In 1905-1906 he made a grand tour of Italy, where he was especially impressed and influenced by Venice.

Returning to Antwerp he became a secretary to the art society of Kunst van Heden/L'Art Contemporain, and worked on the organisation of international exhibitions. Between 1910 and 1912 he lived mainly in Paris. There he had the opportunity to see the exhibition of Italian futurists in 1912 and decided to move to Italy under the impressions of it.

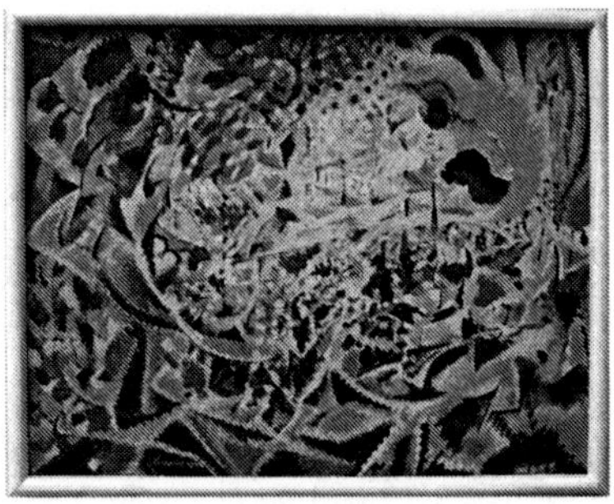

Light

His time in Italy between 1912 and 1914 was the happiest and most active part of his life and art. In 1914 he took part on the international exhibition of futurists in Rome. His style developed towards the abstract.

In 1914 he returned to Antwerp. He was declared unfit for military service on health grounds. After the start of the Great War he moved to The Hague in neutral Netherlands.

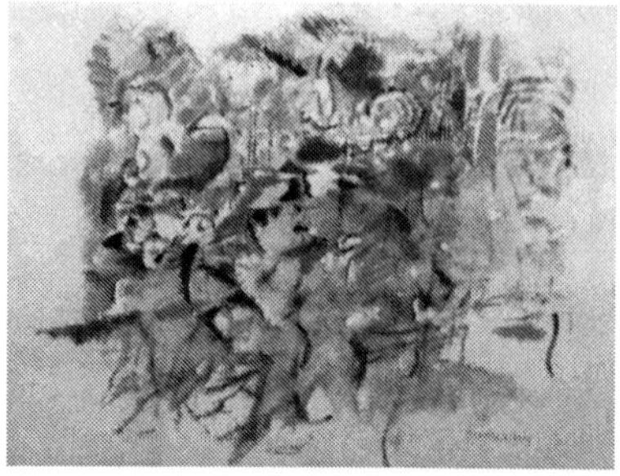

Terrace

He felt lonely in the isolated country, he longed after the sunny Venice and the whirring international life of artists.

In his art he returned to the figurative painting, but his works from this period did not reach the previous level. He fell into depression and committed suicide.

Michael Palmer British art historian has written about him, that Schmalzigaug has not received great acknowledgement in his life neither in Belgium, nor internationally, but in spite of this he belonged to the most original and most talented modern Belgian artists of his time.

His works can be seen in the Royal Museum of Fine Arts, Antwerp, the Royal Museums of Fine Arts of Belgium in Brussels, and the Provincial Museum of Modern Art in Ostend.

Literature

- Phil Mertens, "Jules Schmalzigaug, 1882-1917", Antwerpen en Brussel, 1984
- Michael Palmer, "Van Ensor tot Magritte, Belgische kunst 1880 - 1940", Brussel en Tielt, 2002

Gino Severini

Gino Severini	
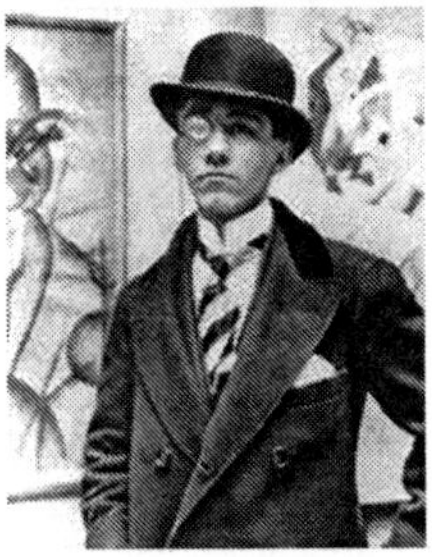 Gino Severini, aged 30, at the opening of his solo exhibition at the Marlborough Gallery, London	
Born	7 April 1883 Cortona, Italy
Died	26 February 1966 (aged 82) Paris
Nationality	Italian
Field	Painting, mosaic, fresco
Training	Rome Fine Art Institute
Movement	Divisionism, Futurism, Cubism, Return to order, Neo-Classicism, Novecento Italiano
Works	*Pan Pan Dance, Dynamic Hieroglyph of the Bal Tabarin, Italian Lancers at a Gallop, Maternity, Conségna delle Chieve*
Awards	Premio Nazionale di Pittura of the Accademia di San Luca, Rome

Gino Severini (7 April 1883–26 February 1966), was an Italian painter and a leading member of the Futurist movement. For much of his life he divided his time between Paris and Rome. He was associated with neo-classicism and the "return to order" in the decade after the First World War. During his career he worked in a variety of media, including mosaic and fresco. He showed his work at major exhibitions, including the Rome Quadrennial, and won art prizes from major institutions.

Early life

Severini was born into a poor family in Cortona, Italy. His father was a junior court official and his mother a dressmaker. He studied at the Scuola Tecnica in Cortona until the age of fifteen, when he was expelled from the entire Italian school system for the theft of exam papers. For a while he worked with his father. Then in 1899 he moved to Rome with his mother. It was there that he first showed a serious interest in art, painting in his spare time while working as a shipping clerk. With the help of a patron of

Cortonese origins he attended art classes, enrolling in the free school for nude studies (an annex of the Rome Fine Art Institute) and a private academy. His formal art education ended after two years when his patron stopped his allowance, declaring, "I absolutely do not understand your lack of order."

In 1900 he met the painter Umberto Boccioni. Together they visited the studio of Giacomo Balla, where they were introduced to the technique of Divisionism, painting with divided rather than mixed color and breaking the painted surface into a field of stippled dots and stripes. The ideas of Divisionism had a great influence on Severini's early work and on Futurist painting from 1910 to 1911.

Severini settled in Paris in November 1906. The move was momentous for him. He said later, "The cities to which I feel most strongly bound are Cortona and Paris: I was born physically in the first, intellectually and spiritually in the second." He lived in Montmartre and dedicated himself to painting. There he met most of the rising artists of the period, befriending Amedeo Modigliani and occupying a studio next to those of Raoul Dufy, George Braque and Suzanne Valadon. He knew most of the Parisian avant-garde, including Juan Gris, Pablo Picasso, Aurélien Lugné-Poë and his theatrical circle, the poets Guillaume Apollinaire, Paul Fort, and Max Jacob, and author Jules Romains. The sale of his work did not provide enough to live on and he depended on the generosity of patrons.

Futurism

He was invited by Filippo Tommaso Marinetti and Boccioni to join the Futurist movement and was a co-signatory, with Balla, Boccioni, Carlo Carrà, and Luigi Russolo, of the *Manifesto of the Futurist Painters* [1] in February 1910 and the *Technical Manifesto of Futurist Painting* [2] in April the same year. He was an important link between artists in France and Italy and came into contact with Cubism before his Futurist colleagues. Following a visit to Paris in 1911, the Italian Futurists adopted a sort of Cubism, which gave them a means of analysing energy in paintings and expressing dynamism. Severini helped to organize the first Futurist exhibition outside Italy at Galerie Bernheim-Jeune, Paris, in February 1912 and participated in subsequent Futurist shows in Europe and the United States. In 1913, he had solo exhibitions at the Marlborough Gallery, London, and Der Sturm, Berlin.

In his autobiography, written many years later, he records that the Futurists were pleased with the response to the exhibition at Galerie Bernheim-Jeune, but that influential critics, notably Apollinaire, mocked them for their pretentions, their ignorance of the main currents of modern art and their provincialism. Severini later came to agree with Apollinaire.

Severini was less attracted to the subject of the machine than his fellow Futurists and frequently chose the form of the dancer to express Futurist theories of dynamism in art. He was particularly adept at rendering lively urban scenes, for example in *Dynamic Hieroglyph of the Bal Tabarin* (1912) and *The Boulevard* (1913). During the First World War he produced some of the finest Futurist war art, notably his *Italian Lancers at a Gallop* (1915) and *Armoured Train* (1915).

Neo-classicism

After 1920 he divided his time between Paris and Rome.

Severini abandoned Futurism after the First World War and was part of the "return to order", becoming interested in a more conservative, analytic type of painting and making a study of Giotto. For a time he worked in a Synthetic Cubist mode, but with the publication of *Du cubisme au classicisme* in 1916 he departed from Cubist purism and adopted a neo-classical style with metaphysical overtones. By 1920 he was applying theories of classical balance based on the Golden Section to figurative subjects from the traditional commedia dell'arte.

In 1923 he took part in the Rome Biennale. He exhibited in Milan with artists of the Novecento Italiano group in 1926 and 1929 and in their Geneva exhibition of 1929. From 1928 he began to incorporate elements of Rome's classical landscape in his work. In 1930 he took part in the Venice Biennale, exhibited in the Rome Quadrennials of 1931 and 1935, and in 1935 won the first prize for painting, with an entire room devoted to his work. He contributed a cycle of works to the Paris Exhibition. He explored fresco and mosaic techniques and executed murals in various media in Switzerland, France, and Italy.

Later life

In the 1940s Severini's style became semi-abstract. In the 1950s he returned to his Futurist subjects: dancers, light and movement. He executed commissions for the church of Saint-Pierre in Freiburg and inaugurated the *Conségna delle Chiavi* ("Delivery of the Keys") mosaic. His mosaics were shown at the Cahiers d'Art gallery in Paris and he participated in a conference on the history of mosaic at Ravenna. He received commissions to decorate the offices of KLM in Rome and Alitalia in Paris and took part in the exhibition *The Futurists, Balla - Severini 1912–1918* at the Rose Fried Gallery in New York. In Rome he reconstructed his *Pan Pan Dance* mosaic, which had been destroyed in the war. He was awarded the *Premio Nazionale di Pittura* of the Accademia di San Luca in Rome, exhibited at the 9th Rome Quadrennal and was given a solo exhibition at the Accademia di San Luca.

Throughout his career he published important theoretical essays and books on art. There is an autobiography, *The Life of a Painter.*

Severini died in Paris on February 26, 1966, aged 82. He was buried at Cortona.

See also

- Futurism
- Art manifesto

References

- Biography of Severini in the Guide to Cortona [3]
- Cowling, Elizabeth; Mundy, Jennifer, *On Classic Ground: Picasso, Léger, de Chirico and the New Classicism 1910–1930*, London: Tate Gallery. ISBN 1-85437-043-X

External links

- MoMA collection, retrieved April 7, 2008 [1]
- *Radical Light* - Exhibition of Divisionist painting at the National Gallery, London [2]

Mario Sironi

Mario Sironi (May 12, 1885 – August 13, 1961) was an Italian modernist artist who was active as a painter, sculptor, illustrator, and designer.

Biography

Born in Sassari on the island of Sardinia, Sironi spent his childhood in Rome. He embarked on the study of engineering at the University of Rome but quit after a nervous breakdown in 1903, one of many severe depressions that would recur throughout his life. Thereafter he dedicated himself to painting, and attended the Scuola Libera del Nudo, where he met Giacomo Balla, Gino Severini and Umberto Boccioni. These artists, who would later become the leading Futurists, were then painting in a Neo-Impressionist style. Sironi's development closely tracked theirs, and he adopted the Futurist style by 1913.

After service in World War I, Sironi's version of Futurism gave way to an art of massive, immobile forms. In paintings such as *La Lampada* of 1919 (Pinateca di Brera, Milan), mannequins substitute for figures, as in the metaphysical paintings of Giorgio de Chirico and Carlo Carrà. Like many artists in the period following the war, Sironi looked to the art af the past for inspiration, and works such as *Venere* of 1921-1923 (Galleria Civica d'Arte Moderna, Turin) and *Solitudine (Solitude)* (Galleria Nazionale d'Arte Moderna, Rome), with their contained, geometric forms, bear some kinship to the neoclassicism evident in works produced at the same time by Picasso. Toward the end of the 1920s, his style became more painterly. Through all of his stylistic developments, Sironi's was always a somber and dramatic vision, characterized by blocky forms, stark oppositions of light and shadow, and a generally pessimistic air.

A supporter of Mussolini, he contributed a large number of cartoons—over 1700 in all—to *Il Popolo d'Italia* and *La Rivista Illustrata del Popola d'Italia*, the Fascist newspapers. Rejecting the art market and the concept of the easel painting, he became committed to the ideal of a fusion of decoration and architecture, as exemplified by Gothic cathedrals. He felt that the mural was the proper basis of a popular national art. The state commissioned from him several large-scale decorative works in the 1930s, such as the mural *L'Italia fra le arti e le scienze (Italy Between the Arts and Sciences)* of 1935, and he also contributed to the Exhibition of the Fascist Revolution in 1932. Although his esthetic of brutal monumentality represented the dominant style of Italian Fascism, his work was attacked by right-wing critics for its lack of overt ideological content.

As an artist closely identified with Fascism, his reputation declined dramatically in the post-World War II period. Embittered by the course of events, he also suffered the loss of his daughter Rossana by suicide in 1948. He had returned to easel painting in 1943, and worked now in relative isolation. The paintings of his later years sometimes approach abstraction, resembling assemblages of archaeological fragments, or juxtaposed sketches. He continued working until shortly before his death in 1961 in Milan.

References

- Baldacci, Paolo, et al. (1989). *Mario Sironi*. Milano: P. Daverio. OCLC 21293509 [1]
- Cowling, Elizabeth; Mundy, Jennifer (1990). *On Classic Ground: Picasso, Léger, de Chirico and the New Classicism 1910-1930*. London: Tate Gallery. ISBN 1-85437-043-X

Ardengo Soffici

Ardengo Soffici (April 7, 1879 – August 12, 1964), was an Italian writer, painter and Fascist intellectual.

Life

Soffici was born in Rignano sull'Arno, near Florence. In 1893 his family moved to the latter city, where he studied at the Accademia from 1897 and later at the Scuola Libera del Nudo.

In 1900 he moved from Florence to Paris, where he lived for seven years, working for Symbolist journals. While in Paris he became acquainted with Braque, Derain, Picasso, Gris and Apollinaire.

On returning to Italy in 1907, Soffici settled in Poggio a Caiano (where he lived for the rest of his life) and wrote articles on modern artists for the first issue of the political and cultural magazine *La Voce*.

In 1910 he organised an exhibition of Impressionist painting in Florence in association with *La Voce*, devoting an entire room to the sculptor Medardo Rosso.

In August 1911 he wrote an article in *La Voce* on Picasso and Braque, which probably influenced the Futurists in the direction of Cubism. At this time Soffici considered Cubism to be an extension of the partial revolution of the Impressionists. In 1912-1913 Soffici painted in a Cubist style.

After visiting the Futurists' Exhibition of Free Art in Milan, he wrote a hostile review in *La Voce*. The leading Futurists Marinetti, Boccioni and Carrà, were so incensed by this that they immediately boarded a train for Florence and assaulted Soffici and his *La Voce* colleagues at the Caffè Giubbe Rosse. Reviewing the Futurists' Paris exhibition of 1912 in his article *Ancora del Futurismo* (Futurism Again) he dismissed their rhetoric, publicity-seeking and their art, but granted that, despite its faults, Futurism was "a movement of renewal, and that is excellent".

Gino Severini was despatched from Milan to Florence to make peace with Soffici on behalf of the Futurists – the Peace of Florence, as Boccioni called it. After these diplomatic overtures, Soffici, together with Giovanni Papini, Aldo Palazzeschi and Italo Tavolato withdrew from *La Voce* in 1913 to form a new periodical, *Lacerba*, which would concentrate entirely on art and culture. Soffici published "Theory of the movement of plastic Futurism" in *Lacerba*, accepting that Futurism had reconciled what had previously seemed irreconcilable, Impressionism and Cubism. By its fifth issue *Lacerba* wholly supported the Futurists. Soffici's paintings in 1913 – e.g. *Linee di una strada* and *Sintesi di una pesaggio autumnale* – showed the influence of the Futurists in method and title and he exhibited with them.

In 1914, personal quarrels and artistic differences between the Milan Futurists and the Florence group around Soffici, Papini and Carlo Carrà, created a rift in Italian Futurism. The Florence group resented the dominance of Marinetti and Boccioni, whom they accused of trying to establish "an immobile church with an infallible creed", and each group dismissed the other as *passéiste*.

After serving in the First World War, Soffici abandoned Futurism and, discovering a new reverence for Tuscan tradition, became associated with the "return to order" which manifested itself in the naturalistic landscapes which threafter dominated his work.

Soffici was one of the signatories of Gentile's 1925 Fascist manifesto. He regarded the United States of America as "false", "transitory" and "ephemeral". It was a "non-civilisation" where the spirituality of art was suffocated by the barbaric vulgarity of a people without history and without tradition, and incapable, therefore, of creating a true civilization. To Soffici and other moralists of Italian Fascism, US civilisation represented "impending modernity", that is to say, a violent negation of the Italian genius; it was necessary to wage a holy war against the American monster to save Italian civilization.

He died at the Italian holiday resort of Forte dei Marmi.

Bibliography

Poems

- *BÏF§ZF+18 = Simultaneità - Chimismi lirici* (1915)
- *Elegia dell'Ambra* (1927)
- *Marsia e Apollo* (1938)
- *Thréne pour Guillame Apollinaire* (1927)

Novels

- *Ignoto toscano* (1909)
- *Lemmonio Boreo* (1912)
- *Arlecchino* (1914)
- *Giornale di bordo* (1915)
- *Kobilek: giornale di battaglia* (1918)
- *La giostra dei sensi* (1918)
- *La ritirata del Friuli* (1919)
- *Rete mediterranea* (1920)
- *Battaglia fra due vittorie* (1923)
- *Ricordi di vita artistica e letteraria* (1931)
- *Taccuino di Arno Borghi* (1933)
- *Ritratto delle cose di Francia* (1934)
- *L'adunata* (1936)
- *Itinerario inglese* (1948)
- *Autoritratto d'artista italiano nel quadro del suo tempo*
    - *L'uva e la croce* (1951)

- *Passi tra le rovine* (1952)
- *Il salto vitale* (1954)
- *Fine di un mondo* (1955)
- *D'ogni erba un fascio* (1958)
- *Diari 1939-1945* (1962, with G. Prezzoloni)

Essays

- *Il caso Rosso e l'impressionismo* (1909)
- *Arthur Rimbaud* (1911)
- *Cubismo e oltre* (1913)
- *Cubismo e futurismo* (1914)
- *Serra e Croce* (1915)
- *Cubismo e futurismo* (1919)
- *Scoperte e massacri* (1919)
- *Primi principi di un'estetica futurista* (1920)
- *Giovanni Fattori* (1921)
- *Armando Spadini* (1925)
- *Carlo Carrà* (1928)
- *Periplo dell'arte* (1928)
- *Medardo Rosso: 1858-1928* (1929)
- *Ugo Bernasconi* (1934)
- *Apollinaire* (1937)
- *Salti nel tempo* (1938)
- *Selva: arte* (1938)
- *Trenta artisti moderni italiani e stranieri* (1950)

References

- Estorick Collection of Modern Italian Art [1]
- Raimondi, Giuseppe; Luigi Cavallo (1967). *Ardengo Soffici*. Florence: Vallecchi.

The Russian Futurists

Vladimir Mayakovsky

Vladimir Mayakovsky	
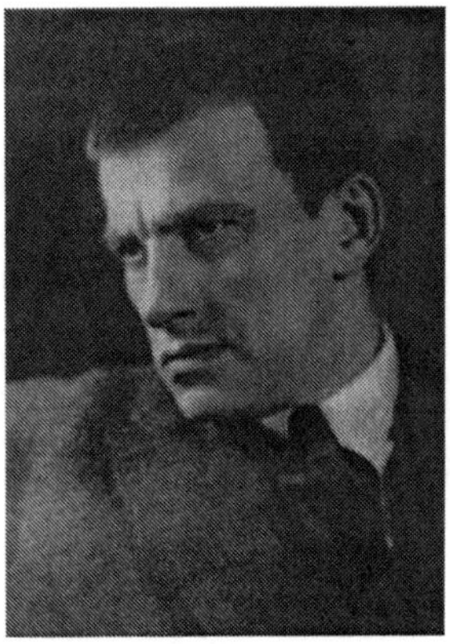	
Born	July 19, 1893 Baghdati, Russian Empire
Died	April 14, 1930 (aged 36) Moscow, USSR
Nationality	Russian
Citizenship	Russian Empire, Soviet
Alma mater	Stroganov Moscow State University of Arts and Industry, Moscow School of Painting, Sculpture and Architecture
Period	1912—1930
Literary movement	Russian Futurism, Cubo-Futurism

Vladimir Vladimirovich Mayakovsky (Влади́мир Влади́мирович Маяко́вский) (July 19 [O.S. July 7] 1893 – April 14, 1930) was a Russian and Soviet poet and playwright, among the foremost representatives of early-20th century Russian Futurism.

Early life

He was born the last of three children in Baghdati, Russian Empire (now in Georgia) where his father worked as a forest ranger. His father was of Ukrainian Cossack descent and his mother was of Ukrainian descent. Although Mayakovsky spoke Georgian at school and with friends, his family spoke primarily Russian at home. At the age of 14 Mayakovsky took part in socialist demonstrations at the town of Kutaisi, where he attended the local grammar school. After the sudden and premature death of his father in 1906, the family — Mayakovsky, his mother, and his two sisters — moved to Moscow, where he attended School No. 5.

In Moscow, Mayakovsky developed a passion for Marxist literature and took part in numerous activities of the Russian Social Democratic Labour Party; he was to later become an RSDLP (Bolshevik) member. In 1908, he was dismissed from the grammar school because his mother was no longer able to afford the tuition fees.

Around this time, Mayakovsky was imprisoned on three occasions for subversive political activities but, being underage, he avoided transportation. During a period of solitary confinement in Butyrka prison in 1909, he began to write poetry, but his poems were confiscated. On his release from prison, he continued working within the socialist movement, and in 1911 he joined the Moscow Art School where he became acquainted with members of the Russian Futurist movement. He became a leading spokesman for the group *Gileas* (Гилея), and a close friend of David Burlyuk, whom he saw as his mentor.

Literary life

The 1912 Futurist publication *A Slap in the Face of Public Taste* (Пощёчина общественному вкусу) contained Mayakovsky's first published poems: *Night* (Ночь) and *Morning* (Утро). Because of their political activities, Burlyuk and Mayakovsky were expelled from the Moscow Art School in 1914.

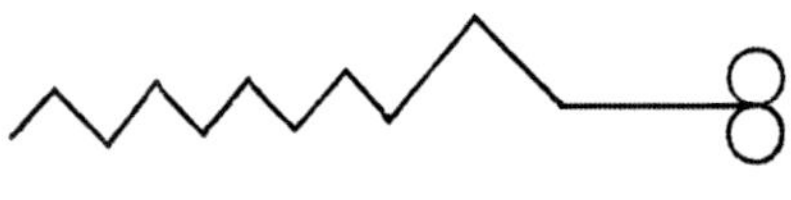

Image from Mayakovsky's *Как делать стихи* ("How to Make Poems").

His work continued in the Futurist vein until 1914. His artistic development then shifted increasingly in the direction of narrative and it was this work, published during the period immediately preceding the Russian Revolution, which was to establish his reputation as a poet in Russia and abroad.

A Cloud in Trousers (1915) was Mayakovsky's first major poem of appreciable length and it depicted the heated subjects of love, revolution, religion and art, written from the vantage point of a spurned lover. The language of the work was the language of the streets, and Mayakovsky went to considerable lengths to debunk idealistic and romanticised notions of poetry and poets.

Your thoughts, *dreaming on a softened brain,* *like an over-fed lackey on a greasy settee,* *with my heart's bloody tatters I'll mock again;* *impudent and caustic, I'll jeer to superfluity.*	Вашу мысль мечтающую на размягченном мозгу, как выжиревший лакей на засаленной кушетке, буду дразнить об окровавленный сердца лоскут: досыта изъиздеваюсь, нахальный и едкий.
Of Grandfatherly gentleness I'm devoid, *there's not a single grey hair in my soul!* *Thundering the world with the might of my voice,* *I go by – handsome,* *twenty-two-year-old.*	У меня в душе ни одного седого волоса, и старческой нежности нет в ней! Мир огромив мощью голоса, иду – красивый, двадцатидвухлетний.

(From the prologue of *A Cloud in Trousers*.)

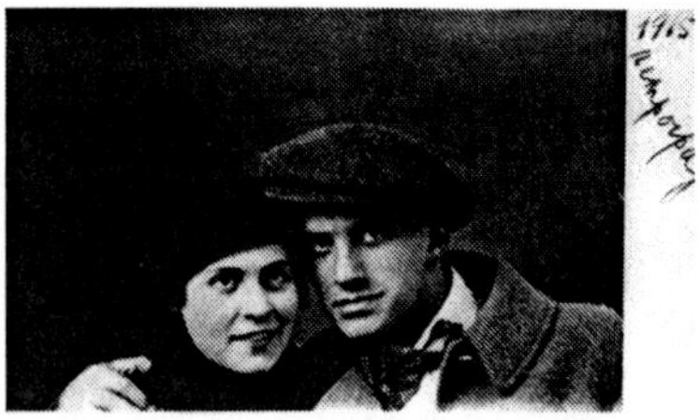

Vladimir Mayakovsky and Lilya Brik.

In the summer of 1915, Mayakovsky fell in love with a married woman, Lilya Brik, and it is to her that the poem "The Backbone Flute" (1916) was dedicated; unfortunately for Mayakovsky, she was the wife of his publisher, Osip Brik. The love affair, as well as his impressions of war and revolution, strongly influenced his works of these years. The poem "War and the World" (1916) addressed the horrors of WWI and "Man" (1917) is a poem dealing with the anguish of love.

Mayakovsky was rejected as a volunteer at the beginning of WWI, and during 1915-1917 worked at the Petrograd Military Automobile School as a draftsman. At the onset of the Russian Revolution, Mayakovsky was in Smolny, Petrograd. There he witnessed the October Revolution. He started reciting poems such as "Left March! For the Red Marines: 1918" (Левый марш (Матросам), 1918) at naval theatres, with sailors as an audience.

His satirical play *Mystery-Bouffe* was staged in 1918, and again, more successfully, in 1921.

After moving back to Moscow, Mayakovsky worked for the Russian State Telegraph Agency (ROSTA) creating — both graphic and text — satirical Agitprop posters. In 1919, he published his first collection of poems *Collected Works 1909-1919* (Все сочиненное Владимиром Маяковским). In the cultural climate of the early Soviet Union, his popularity grew rapidly. From 1922 to 1928, Mayakovsky was a prominent member of the Left Art Front and went on to define his work as 'Communist futurism' (комфут). He edited, along with Sergei Tretyakov and Osip Brik, the journal LEF.

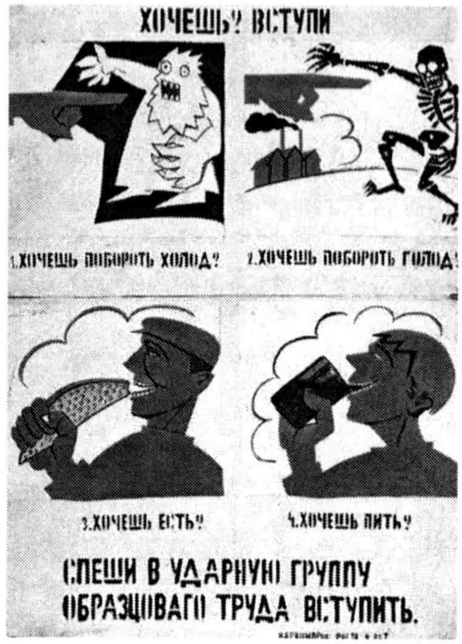

Agitprop poster by Mayakovsky

As one of the few Soviet writers who were allowed to travel freely, his voyages to Latvia, Britain, Germany, the United States, Mexico and Cuba influenced works like *My Discovery of America* (Мое открытие Америки, 1925). He also travelled extensively throughout the Soviet Union.

On a lecture tour in the United States, Mayakovsky met Elli Jones, who later gave birth to his daughter, an event which Mayakovsky only came to know in 1929, when the couple met clandestinely in the south of France, as the relationship was kept secret. In the late 1920s, Mayakovsky fell in love with Tatiana Yakovleva and to her he dedicated the poem "A Letter to Tatiana Yakovleva" (Письмо Татьяне Яковлевой, 1928).

The relevance of Mayakovsky's influence cannot be limited to Soviet poetry. While for years he was considered the Soviet poet par excellence, he also changed the perceptions of poetry in wider 20th century culture. His political activism as a propagandistic agitator was rarely understood and often looked upon unfavourably by contemporaries, even close friends like Boris Pasternak. Near the end of the 1920s, Mayakovsky became increasingly disillusioned with the course the Soviet Union was taking under Joseph Stalin: his satirical plays *The Bedbug* (Клоп, 1929) and *The Bathhouse* (Баня, 1930), which deal with the Soviet philistinism and bureaucracy, illustrate this development.

On the evening of April 14, 1930, Mayakovsky shot himself. The *unfinished poem* in his suicide note read, in part:

And so they say-
"the incident dissolved"
the love boat smashed up
on the dreary routine.
I'm through with life
and [we] should absolve
from mutual hurts, afflictions and
spleen.

Mayakovsky was interred at the Moscow Novodevichy Cemetery.

After his death

In 1930, his birthplace of Bagdadi in Georgia was renamed Mayakovsky in his honour. After his death, Mayakovsky was attacked in the Soviet press as a "formalist" and a "fellow-traveller" (попутчик) (as opposed to officially recognised "proletarian poets", such as Demyan Bedny). When, in 1935, Lilya Brik wrote to Stalin to complain about the attacks, Stalin wrote a comment on Brik's letter:

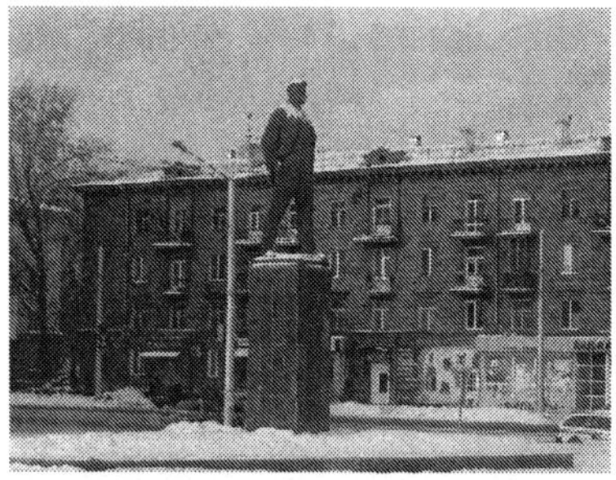

Mayakovsky statue in Novokuznetsk

> "Comrade Yezhov, please take charge of Brik's letter. Mayakovsky is still the best and the most talented poet of our Soviet epoch. Indifference to his cultural heritage is a crime. Brik's complaints are, in my opinion, justified..."

These words became a cliché and officially canonized Mayakovsky but, as Boris Pasternak noted, they "dealt him the second death" in some circles.

In 1938 the Mayakovskaya Metro Station was opened to the public, demonstrating various innovations architecture- and design-wise, among them the display of ceiling mosaics that resemble a "fish-eye" view from the underground to the Moscow sky.

Yevgeny Yevtushenko once said *As a poet, I wanted to mix something from Mayakovsky and Yesenin.* Mayakovsky was, however, the most influential futurist in Lithuania and his poetry helped to form the *Four Winds* movement there. He was also an influence on the writer Valentin Kataev. Andrey Voznesensky called Mayakovsky teacher and favorite poet and dedicated him a poem *Маяковский в Париже* (*Mayakovsky in Paris*). In 1967 the Taganka Theater staged the poetical performance *Послушайте!*, based on Mayakovsky's works. Role of the poet was played by Vladimir Vysotsky, who also was inspired by Mayakovsky's poetry.

In 1974 a Russian State Museum of Mayakovsky was opened in the center of Moscow in the building where Mayakovsky resided from 1919 to 1930. Vladimir Mayakovsky and his works were a major influence on the work of Italian actor, film director and screenwriter Carmelo Bene, who interpreted Mayakovsky on the stages of theatres in Italy and on TV from the early 1970s until his death in 2002. Frank O'Hara wrote a poem named after him, "Mayakovsky" in which the speaker is standing in a bathtub, a probable reference to his play "The Bathhouse". In 1981 Brazilian singer Gal Costa recorded "O Amor" a Portuguese version of one of Mayakovsky's latter poems in her album *Fantasia*. In 1986 English singer and songwriter Billy Bragg recorded the album Talking with the Taxman about Poetry, named after a namesake Mayakovsky's poem. In 1991, City Lights published *Listen! Early Poems*, a collection translated by Maria Enzensberger. The well-known phrase "Lenin lives, lived and will live" comes from his elegy "Vladimir Ilyich Lenin".

In 2005 the north exit of the Mayakovskaya Metro Station was opened, referencing the architecture of the underground station with ample sculpturing of marble, stainless steel and another group of ceiling mosaic works, accompanied by the artist's poems. In 2009, Italian alternative rock band, Il Teatro Degli Orrori, released a song entitled "Majakowskij". The lyrics of the song are the Italian translation of his 1916 poem *To His Beloved Self, the Author Dedicates these Lines* (Себе любимому посвещает эти строки автор). In 2010, in collaboration with Found Reality Theatre, students at the University of Glamorgan staged a physical theatre piece entitled The Mayakovsky Project in the Atrium, Cardiff. Using Mayakovsky's life as template, the performance posed the question, "Why do they kill the artists?"[citation needed]

References

Bibliography

- Aizlewood, Robin. *Verse form and meaning in the poetry of Vladimir Maiakovsky: Tragediia, Oblako v shtanakh, Fleita-pozvonochnik, Chelovek, Liubliu, Pro eto* (Modern Humanities Research Association, London, 1989).
- Brown, E. J. *Mayakovsky: a poet in the revolution* (Princeton Univ. Press, 1973).
- Charters, Ann & Samuel. *I love : the story of Vladimir Mayakovsky and Lili Brik* (Farrar Straus Giroux, NY, 1979).
- Humesky, Assya. *Majakovskiy and his neologisms* (Rausen Publishers, NY, 1964).
- Jangfeldt, Bengt. *Majakovsky and futurism 1917-1921* (Almqvist & Wiksell International, Stockholm, 1976).
- Lavrin, Janko. *From Pushkin to Mayakovsky, a study in the evolution of a literature.* (Sylvan Press, London, 1948).
- Mayakovsky, Vladimir (Patricia Blake ed., trans. Max Hayward and George Reavey). *The bedbug and selected poetry.* (Meridian Books, Cleveland, 1960).
- Mayakovsky, Vladimir. *Mayakovsky: Plays.* Trans. Guy Daniels. (Northwestern University Press, Evanston, Il, 1995). ISBN 0810113392.
- Mayakovsky, Vladimir. *For the voice* (The British Library, London, 2000).
- Mayakovsky, Vladimir (ed. Bengt Jangfeldt, trans. Julian Graffy). *Love is the heart of everything : correspondence between Vladimir Mayakovsky and Lili Brik 1915-1930* (Polygon Books, Edinburgh, 1986).
- Mayakovsky, Vladimir (comp. and trans. Herbert Marshall). *Mayakovsky and his poetry* (Current Book House, Bombay, 1955).
- Mayakovsky, Vladimir. *Selected works in three volumes* (Raduga, Moscow, 1985).
- Mayakovsky, Vladimir. *Selected poetry.* (Foreign Languages, Moscow, 1975).

- Mayakovsky, Vladimir (ed. Bengt Jangfeldt and Nils Ake Nilsson). *Vladimir Majakovsky: Memoirs and essays* (Almqvist & Wiksell Int., Stockholm 1975).
- Mayakovsky, Vladimir. *Satira* ('Khudozh. lit.,' Moscow, 1969).
- Mikhailov, Aleksandr Alekseevich. *Maiakovskii* (Mol. gvardiia, Moscow, 1988).
- Novatorskoe iskusstvo Vladimira Maiakovskogo (trans. Alex Miller). *Vladimir Mayakovsky: Innovator* (Progress Publishers, Moscow, 1976).
- Noyes, George R. *Masterpieces of the Russian drama* (Dover Pub., NY, 1960).
- Nyka-Niliūnas, Alfonsas. *Keturi vėjai ir keturvėjinikai* (The Four Winds literary movement and its members), *Aidai*, 1949, No. 24. (Lithuanian)
- Rougle, Charles. *Three Russians consider America : America in the works of Maksim Gorkij, Aleksandr Blok, and Vladimir Majakovsky* (Almqvist & Wiksell International, Stockholm, 1976).
- Shklovskii, Viktor Borisovich. (ed. and trans. Lily Feiler). *Mayakovsky and his circle* (Dodd, Mead, NY, 1972).
- Stapanian, Juliette. *Mayakovsky's cubo-futurist vision* (Rice University Press, 1986).
- Terras, Victor. *Vladimir Mayakovsky* (Twayne, Boston, 1983).
- Vallejo, César (trans. Richard Schaaf) *The Mayakovsky case* (Curbstone Press, Willimantic, CT, 1982).
- Wachtel, Michael. *The development of Russian verse : meter and its meanings* (Cambridge University Press, 1998).

External links

- Biography [1]
- State Museum of Mayakovsky [2] in Moscow (Russian/English)
- Audio introduction, in English, to Mayakovsky's poems. Includes links. [3]
- Between Agitation and Animation: Activism and Participation in Twentieth Century Art by Stella Rollig [4]
- Radio Mayakovsky [5] More than 100 new songs written to the Mayakovsky verses. Mayakovsky Voice, Verses Readers and other stuff
- Vladimir Mayakovsky's Gravesite [6]
- "Баня" ("The Bathhouse"): Mayakovsky and Meyerhold) [7]
- Meyerhold & Mayakovsky - Biomechanics & the Communist Utopia [8]
- The 'raging bull' of Russian poetry [9] article by Dalia Karpel at Haaretz.com, published on-line July 5, 2007
- Archival film edited by Copernicus Films [10]
- English translations of *Take that! (Наme!)* [11], *The love boat smashed up on the dreary routine... (Любовная лодка разбилась о быт)* [12].
- Chapter on Russian Futurists incl Mayakovsky in Trotsky's Literature and Revolution [13]

- Mayakovsky in the Soviet fine arts [14]
- English translations of 3 poems from 1913 [15]
- English translation of ***I*** by Alex Cigale [16]
- English translations of 3 film treatments c. 1918 by Alex Cigale [17]

Mikhail Larionov

Mikhail Fyodorovich Larionov (Russian: **Михаи́л Фёдорович Ларио́нов**, June 3, 1881 – May 10, 1964) was an avant-garde Russian painter.

Life and work

Mikhail Larionov was born at Tiraspol, near Odessa. In 1898 he entered the Moscow School of Painting, Sculpture and Architecture under Isaac Levitan and Valentin Serov. He was suspended three times for his radical outlook. In 1900 he met Natalya Sergeevna Goncharova and formed a life-long relationship with her.

From 1902 his style was Impressionism. After a visit to Paris in 1906 he moved into Post-Impressionism and then a Neo-primitive style which derived partly from Russian sign painting. In 1908 he staged the Golden Fleece exhibition in Moscow, which included paintings by international avant-garde artists such as Matisse, Derain, Braque, Gauguin and Van Gogh. Other group shows promoted by him included Tatlin, Chagall and Malevich.

Larionov was a founding member of two important Russian artistic groups Jack of Diamonds (1909–1911) and the more radical Donkey's Tail (1912–1913). He gave names to both groups. His first solo show was for one day in Moscow in 1911.

In 1913 he created Rayonism, which was the first creation of near-abstract art in Russia. In 1915 he left Russia and worked with the ballet owner Sergei Diaghilev in Paris on the productions of the Ballets Russes.

In 2001, the Central Bank of Transnistria minted a silver coin honoring this native of today's Transnistria, as part of a series of memorable coins called *The Outstanding People of Pridnestrovie.*

The highest price paid for a Larionov painting at auction is 2,200,000 British pounds.[1]

External links

- Online gallery of Larionov paintings [2]
- Marevna, "Smokers" [3] showing Ballet owner Serge de Diaghilev (centre) with Jean Cocteau (to his left), Natalya Goncharova (left) and her husband Mikhail Larionov (right), (scroll down to 3rd painting).

Natalia Goncharova

Natalia Goncharova	
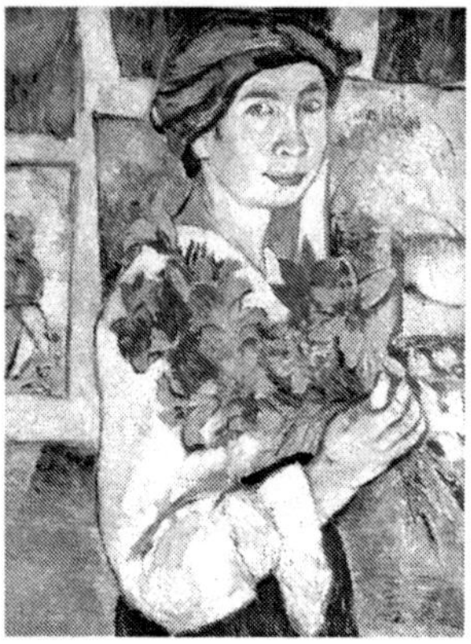 Self Portrait with Yellow Lilies. 1907	
Nationality	Russian
Field	Painting, Costume design, writer, illustrator, set designer

Natalia Sergeevna Goncharova (Russian: Ната́лья Серге́евна Гончаро́ва; June 4, 1881 - October 17, 1962) was a Russian avant-garde artist (Cubo-Futurism), painter, costume designer, writer, illustrator, and set designer. Her great-aunt was Natalia Pushkina, wife of the poet Alexander Pushkin.

Life and work

Natalia Goncharova was born in Nagaevo village near Tula, Russia in 1881. She studied sculpture at the Moscow Academy of Art, but turned to painting in 1904. She was deeply inspired by the primitive aspects of Russian folk art and attempted to emulate it in her own work while incorporating elements of fauvism and cubism. Together with her husband Mikhail Larionov she first developed Rayonism. They were the main progenitors of the pre-Revolution Russian avant-garde organising the Donkey's Tail exhibition of 1912 and showing with the Der Blaue Reiter in Munich the same year.

The Donkey's Tail was conceived as an intentional break from European art influence and the establishment of an independent Russian school of modern art. However, the influence of Russian Futurism is much in evidence in Goncharova's later paintings. Initially preoccupied with icon painting and the primitivism of ethnic Russian folk-art, Goncharova became famous in Russia for her Futurist work such as *The Cyclist* and her later Rayonnist works. As leaders of the Moscow Futurists, they organised provocative lecture evenings in the same vein as their Italian counterparts. Goncharova was also involved with graphic design - writing and illustrating a book in Futurist style.

Goncharova was a member of the Der Blaue Reiter avant-garde group from its founding in 1911. In 1915, she began to design ballet costumes and sets in Geneva. Her designs for the ballet Liturgy: Six Winged Seraph,Angel, St. Andrew, St. Mark, Nativity etc. were started in 1915. The Liturgy was commissioned by Diaghilev with Goncharova, Léonide Massine and Igor Stravinsky. She moved to Paris in 1921 where she designed a number of stage sets of Sergei Diaghilev's Ballets Russes. She became a French citizen in 1939.

In 1962 she died in Paris.

Legacy

On June 18, 2007 Goncharova's 1909 painting *Picking Apples* was auctioned at Christie's for $9.8 million, setting a record for any female artist. The record was updated a year later, when Goncharova's 1912 still-life *The Flowers* (formerly part of Guillaume Apollinaire's collection) sold for $10.8 million.

External links

- Information on Goncharova [1]
- Natalia Goncharova Website [2]

Kazimir Malevich

Kazimir Malevich	
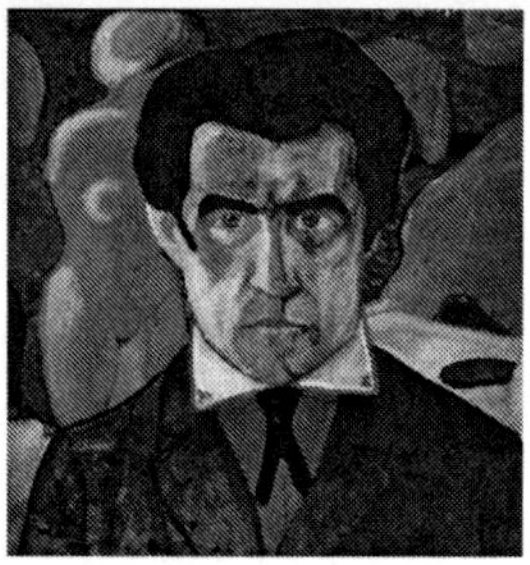 Self-Portrait, 1912	
Birth name	Kazimir Severinovich Malevich
Born	23 February 1879 Kiev Governorate of Russian Empire
Died	15 May 1935 (aged 57) Leningrad, Soviet Union
Nationality	Russian Empire, Soviet Union
Field	Painting
Training	Moscow School of Painting, Sculpture and Architecture
Movement	Suprematism
Works	*Black Square*, 1913; *White on White*, 1918

Kazimir Severinovich Malevich (Russian: Казимир Северинович Малевич, Polish: *Kazimierz Malewicz*, Ukrainian: Казимир Северинович Малевич Ukrainian pronunciation: [kazɪˈmɪr sɛʋɛˈrɪnoʋɪtʃ mɑˈlɛʋɪtʃ], German: *Kasimir Malewitsch*, Belarusian: Казімéр Малéвіч), (February 23, 1879, previously 1878: see below – May 15, 1935) was a Russian painter and art theoretician, born in Ukraine of ethnic Polish parents. He was a pioneer of geometric abstract art and the originator of the Avant-garde Suprematist movement.

Life and work

Kazimir Malevich was born near Kyiv in the Kyiv Governorate of the Russian Empire. His parents, Seweryn and Ludwika Malewicz, were ethnic Poles, and he was baptised in the Roman Catholic Church. His father was the manager of a sugar factory. Kazimir was the first of fourteen children, although only nine of the children survived into adulthood. His family moved often and he spent most childhood in the villages of Ukraine amidst sugar-beet plantations, far from centers of culture. Until age 12 he knew nothing of professional artists, though art had surrounded him in childhood. He delighted in peasant embroidery, and in decorated walls and stoves. He himself was able to paint in the peasant style. He studied drawing in Kyiv from 1895 to 1896.

Black Square, 1913, Oil on Canvas, State Russian Museum, St.Petersburg

From 1896 to 1904 Kazimir Malevich lived in Kursk. In 1904, after the death of his father, he moved to Moscow. He studied at the Moscow School of Painting, Sculpture and Architecture from 1904 to 1910 and in the studio of Fedor Rerberg in Moscow (1904–1910). In 1911 he participated in the second exhibition of the group *Soyuz Molodyozhi* (Union of Youth) in St. Petersburg, together with Vladimir Tatlin and, in 1912, the group held its third exhibition, which included works by Aleksandra Ekster, Tatlin and others. In the same year he participated in an exhibition by the collective *Donkey's Tail* in Moscow. By that time his works were influenced by Natalia Goncharova and Mikhail Larionov, Russian avant-garde painters who were particularly interested in Russian folk art called *lubok*. In March 1913 a major exhibition of Aristarkh Lentulov's paintings opened in Moscow. The effect of this exhibition was comparable with that of Paul Cézanne in Paris in 1907, as all the main Russian avant-garde artists of the time (including Malevich) immediately absorbed the cubist principles and began using them in their works. Already in the same year the Cubo-Futurist opera *Victory Over the Sun* with Malevich's stage-set became a great success. In 1914 Malevich exhibited his works in the *Salon des Independants* in Paris together with Alexander Archipenko, Sonia Delaunay, Aleksandra Ekster and Vadim Meller, among others.

In 1915, Malevich laid down the foundations of Suprematism. He published his manifesto *From Cubism to Suprematism*. In 1915-1916 he worked with other Suprematist artists in a peasant/artisan co-operative in Skoptsi and Verbovka village. In 1916-1917 he participated in exhibitions of the *Jack of Diamonds* group in Moscow together with Nathan Altman, David Burliuk and A. Ekster, among others. Famous examples of his Suprematist works include *Black Square* (1913) and *White on White* (1918).

In 1918, Malevich decorated a play, *Mystery Bouffe*, by Vladimir Mayakovskiy produced by Vsevolod Meyerhold.

He was also interested in aerial photography and aviation, which led him to abstractions inspired by or derived from aerial landscapes. As Professor Julia Bekman Chadaga (now of Macalaster College [1]) has written: "In his later writings, Malevich defined the 'additional element' as the quality of any new visual environment bringing about a change in perception .... In a series of diagrams illustrating the 'environments' that influence various painterly styles, the Suprematist is associated with a series of aerial views rendering the familiar landscape into an abstraction..." (excerpted from Ms. Bekman Chadaga's paper delivered at Columbia University's 2000 symposium, "Art, Technology, and Modernity in Russia and Eastern Europe").

After the October Revolution, Malevich became a member of the Collegium on the Arts of Narkompros, the commission for the protection of monuments and the museums commission (all from 1918–1919). He taught at the Vitebsk Practical Art School in the USSR (now part of Belarus) (1919–1922), the Leningrad Academy of Arts (1922–1927), the Kyiv State Art Institute (1927–1929), and the House of the Arts in Leningrad (1930). He wrote the book *The World as Non-Objectivity* (Munich 1926; English trans. 1959) which outlines his Suprematist theories.

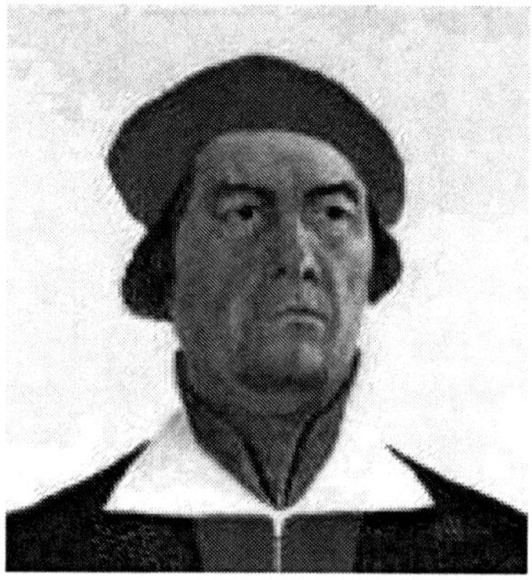

Self-portrait, 1933 (detail)

In 1927, he traveled to Warsaw and then to Berlin and Munich for a retrospective which finally brought him international recognition. He arranged to leave most of the paintings behind when he returned to the Soviet Union. Malevich's assumption that a shifting in the attitudes of the Soviet authorities towards the modernist art movement would take place after the death of Lenin and Trotsky's fall from power, were proven correct in a couple of years, when the Stalinist regime turned against formes of abstractism, considering them a type of "bourgeois" art, that could not express social realities. As a consequence, many of his works were confiscated and he was banned from creating and exhibiting similar art.

Critics derided Malevich for reaching art by negating everything good and pure: love of life and love of nature. The Westernizer artist and art historian Alexandre Benois was one such critic. Malevich responded that art can advance and develop for art's sake alone, regardless of its pleasure: art does not need us, and it never did.

Malevich's work only recently reappeared in art exhibitions in Russia after a long absence. Since then art followers have labored to reintroduce the artist to Russian lovers of painting. A book of his theoretical works with an anthology of reminiscences and writings has been published.

Malevich died of cancer in Leningrad on May 15, 1935. On his deathbed he was exhibited with the black square above him. His ashes were sent to Nemchinovka, and buried in a field near his dacha. A white cube decorated with a black square was placed on his tomb. The city of Leningrad bestowed a pension on Malevich's mother and daughter. "No phenomenon is mortal," Malevich wrote in an unpublished manuscript, "and this means not only the body but the idea as well, a symbol that one is eternally reincarnated in another form which actually exists in the conscious and unconscious person."

Date of birth

Recently Ukrainian art historians established the precise birthdate of the artist: February 23, 1879. *Malevich and Ukraine,* by professor D. Gorbachev, 2006, Kiev, reveals many new biographical details. French art historian Andrei Nakov re-established Malevich's birth year as 1879 (and not 1878), and argues for restoration of the Polish spelling of his name.

Posthumous sales

Black Square, the fourth version of his magnum opus painted in the 1920s was discovered in 1993 in Samara and purchased by Inkombank for $250,000. In April 2002 the painting was auctioned for an equivalent of one million dollars. The purchase was financed by the Russian philanthropist Vladimir Potanin, who donated funds to Russian Ministry of Culture and ultimately to State Hermitage Museum collection. According to the Hermitage website, this was the largest private contribution to state art museums since the October Revolution.

On November 3, 2008 a work by Malevich entitled *Suprematist Composition* from 1916 set the world record for any Russian work of art and any work sold at auction for that year, selling at Sotheby's in New York City for just over $60 million U.S. (far surpassing his previous record of $17 million set in 2000).

Malevich in popular culture

- The smuggling of Malevich paintings out of Russia is a key to the plot line of Martin Cruz Smith's thriller *Red Square*.
- Noah Charney's novel, *The Art Thief* tells the story of two stolen Malevich White on White paintings, and discusses the implications of Malevich's radical Suprematist compositions on the art world.

Selected works

- 1912 *Morning in the Country after Snowstorm*
- 1912 *The Woodcutter*
- 1912-13 *Reaper on Red Background*
- 1914 *The Aviator*
- 1914 *An Englishman in Moscow*
- 1914 *Soldier of the First Division*
- 1915 *Black Square and Red Square*
- 1915 *Red Square: Painterly Realism of a Peasant Woman in Two Dimensions*
- 1915 *Suprematist Composition*
- 1915 *Suprematism (1915)*
- 1915 *Suprematist Painting: Aeroplane Flying*
- 1915 *Suprematism: Self-Portrait in Two Dimensions*
- 1915-16 *Suprematist Painting (Ludwigshafen)*
- 1916 *Suprematist Painting (1916)*
- 1916 *Supremus No. 56*
- 1916-17 *Suprematism (1916–17)*
- 1917 *Suprematist Painting (1917)*
- 1928-32 *Complex Presentiment: Half-Figure in a Yellow Shirt*
- 1932-34 *Running Man*

Gallery

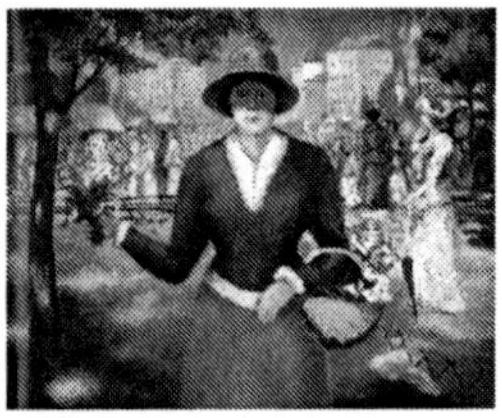
Flower Girl, 1903

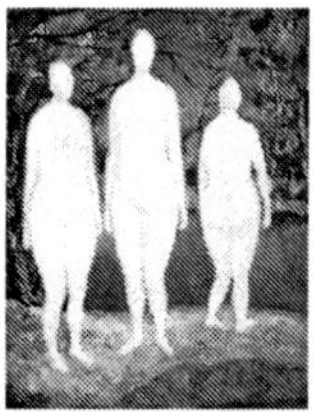
Bathers, 1908

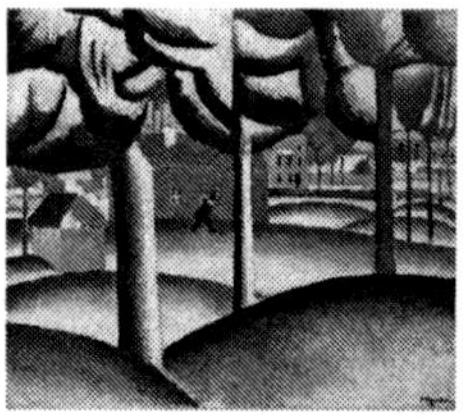
Winter, 1909

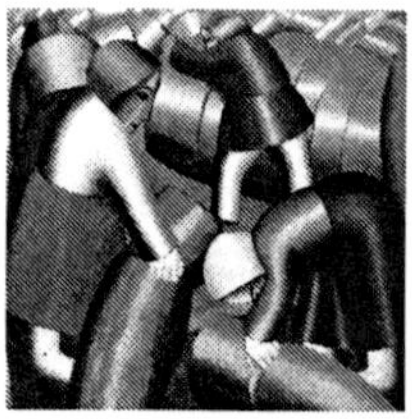
Taking in the Rye, 1911

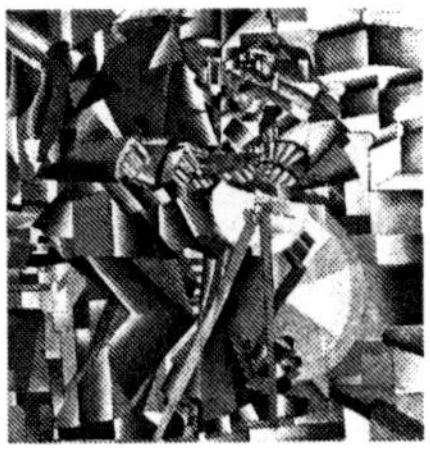
The Knifegrinder, 1912

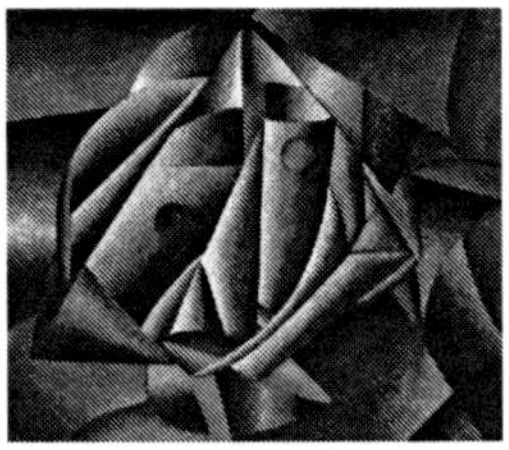
Head of a Peasant Girl, 1912-1913

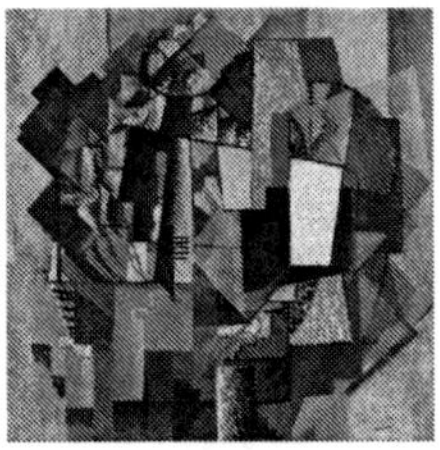
Bureau and Room, 1913

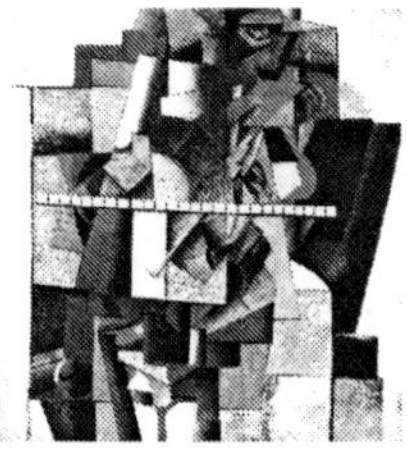
Portrait of Matiushin, 1913

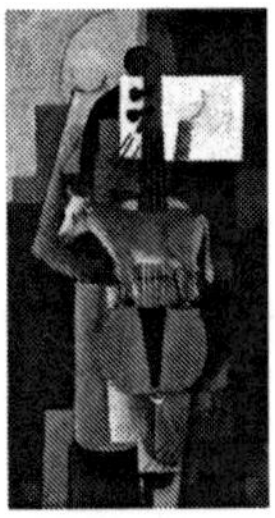
Cow and Fiddle, 1913

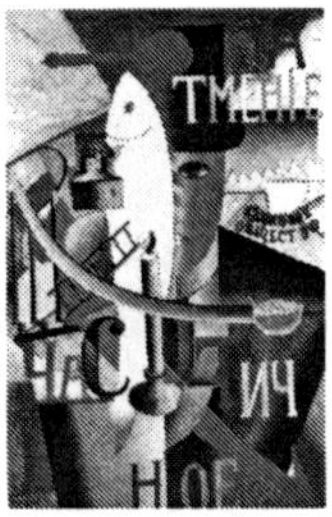
Englishman in Moscow, 1914

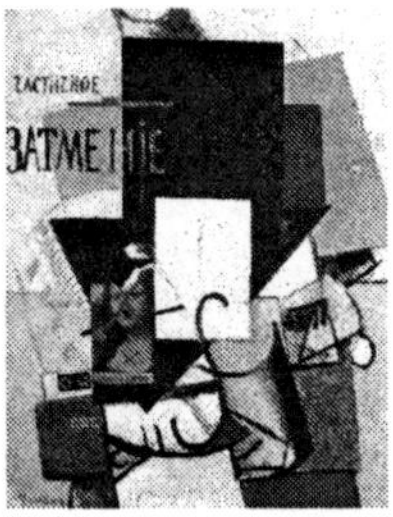
Composition with the Mona Lisa, 1914

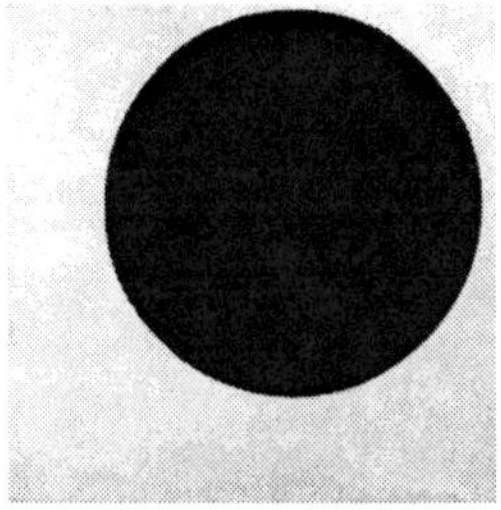
Black Circle, signed 1913, painted 1915

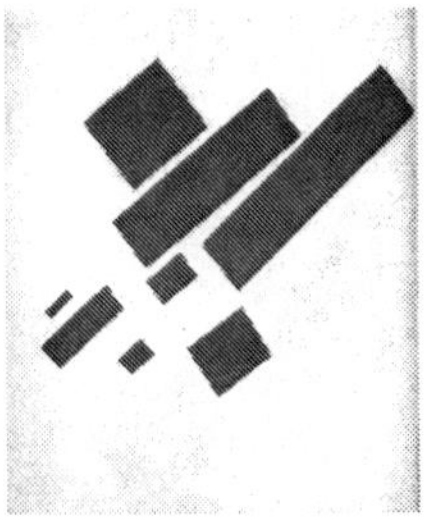
Suprematism (Self-Portrait), 1916

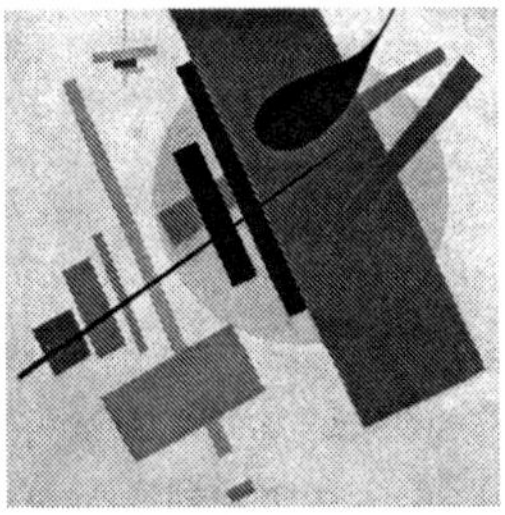
Suprematism, Museum of Art, Krasnodar 1916

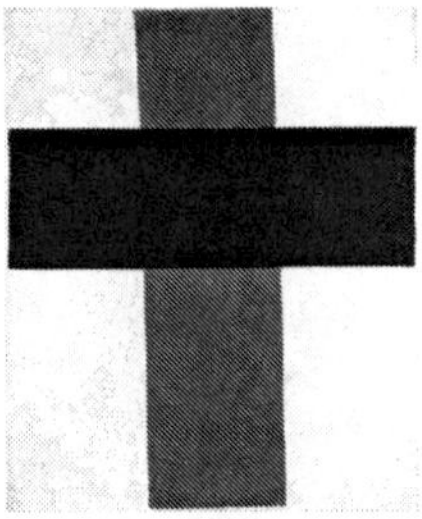
Suprematism, 1921-1927

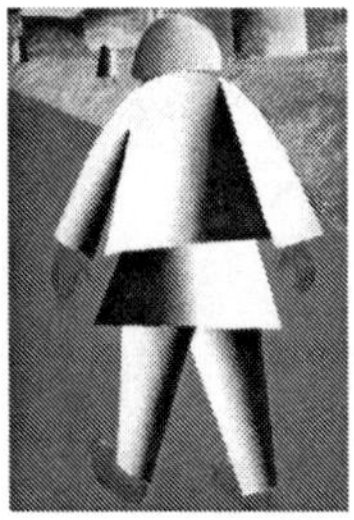
Boy, 1928-1932

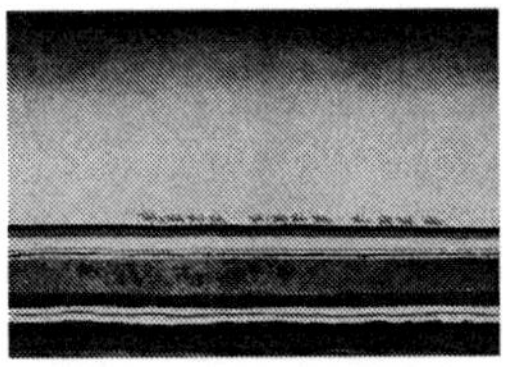
Red-cavalry, 1928-1932

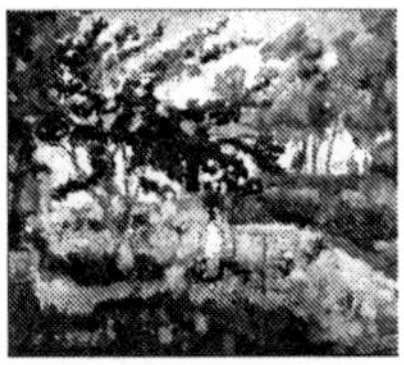
Summer Landscape, 1929

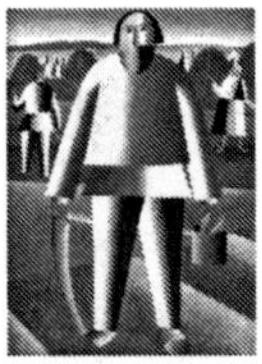
Mower, 1930

See also

- Aerial landscape art
- El Lissitzky
- IRWIN
- Lyubov Popova
- OBERIU
- Rabo Karabekian
- Suprematism
- Supremus
- UNOVIS

References

- Andrei Nakov *Kasimir Malevich, Catalogue raisonné*, Paris, Adam Biro, 2002
- Andrei Nakov vol. IV of *Kasimir Malevich, le peintre absolu*, Paris, Thalia Édition, 2007
- *The Non-objective World*, Kasimir Malevich, trans. Howard Dearstyne, Paul Theobald, 1959. ISBN 0486429741
- *Kazimir Malevich and Suprematism 1878-1935*, Gilles Néret, Taschen, 2003. ISBN 0874141192
- Dreikausen, Margret, "Aerial Perception: The Earth as Seen from Aircraft and Spacecraft and Its Influence on Contemporary Art" (Associated University Presses: Cranbury, NJ; London, England; Mississauga, Ontario: 1985). ISBN 0-87982-040-3
- Milner, John; Malevich, Kazimir, *Kazimir Malevich and the art of geometry*, Yale University Press, 1966. ISBN 0300064179
- Shishanov V.A. *Vitebsk Museum of Modern Art: a history of creation and a collection.* 1918–1941. - Minsk: Medisont, 2007. - 144 p. *Mylivepage.ru* [2]
- *Kazimir Malevich in the State Russian Museum*. Palace Editions. ISBN 978-3930775767. (English Edition)
- *Malevich and his Influence*, Kunstmuseum Liechtenstein, 2008. ISBN 978-3-7757-1877-6
- Ivanov, Sergei."Unknown Socialist Realism. The Leningrad School". Saint Petersburg: NP-Print, 2007, ISBN13 9785901724217 [3]

External links and references

- All Paintings of Kazimir Malevich [4]
- Andrei Nakov's works on Kazimir Malevich [5]
- Guggenheim: Kazimir Malevich [6]
- "White on White" [7]
- DA Collection [8]
- Kazimir-Malevich.org - 128 works by Kazimir Malevich [9]
- "Victory Over the Sun" discussed [10]
- Das schwarze quadrat (The Black Square) - Exhibition at Kunsthalle Hamburg [11]
- Lawsuit over ownership of Malevich's Paintings Settled [12]
- Less known paintings and photographs from private collection [8]
- Sergei V. Ivanov. The Leningrad School of painting. Historical outline [13]
- Kazimir Malevich Website [14]

Velimir Khlebnikov

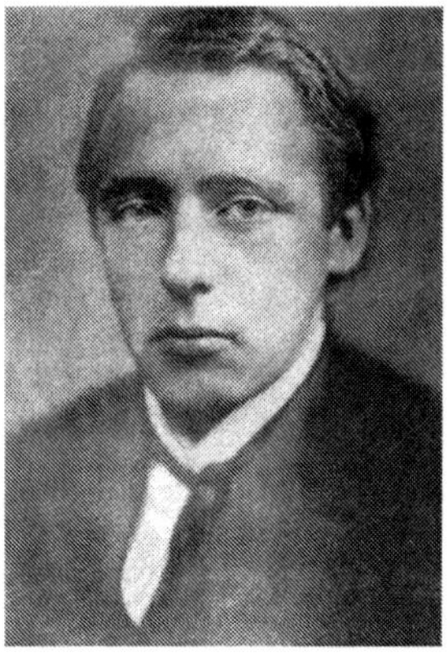

Born	Viktor Vladimirovich Khlebnikov 9 November [O.S. 28 October] 1885 Malye Derbety, Russian Empire
Died	June 28, 1922 (aged 36) Kresttsy, USSR
Pen name	Velimir Khlebnikov
Nationality	Russian
Literary movement	Russian Futurism

Velimir Khlebnikov (Russian: Велими́р Хле́бников; first name also spelled Velemir; last name also spelled Chlebnikov, Hlebnikov, Xlebnikov), pseudonym of **Viktor Vladimirovich Khlebnikov** (9 November 1885 (28 October 1885 (O.S.)) – 28 June 1922), was a central part of the Russian Futurist movement, but his work and influence stretch far beyond it.

Khlebnikov belonged to the most significant Russian Futurist group Hylaea (along with Vladimir Mayakovsky, Aleksei Kruchenykh, David Burliuk, and Benedikt Livshits), but had already written many significant poems before the Futurist movement in Russia had taken shape. Among his contemporaries, he was regarded as "a poet's poet" (Mayakovsky referred to him as a "poet for producers") and a maverick genius.

Khlebnikov is known for poems such as "Incantation by Laughter", "Bobeobi Sang The Lips", "The Grasshopper" (all 1908-9), "Snake Train" (1910), the prologue to the Futurist opera *Victory over the Sun* (1913), dramatic works such as "Death's Mistake" (1915), prose works "Ka" (1915), and the so-called 'super-tale' (сверхповесть) "Zangezi", a sort of ecstatic drama written partly in invented languages of gods and birds.

In his work, Khlebnikov experimented with the Russian language, drawing upon its roots to invent huge numbers of neologisms, and finding significance in the shapes and sounds of individual letters of the Cyrillic alphabet. Along with Kruchenykh, he originated zaum.

He wrote futurological essays about such things as the possible evolution of mass communication ("The Radio of the Future") and transportation and housing ("Ourselves and Our Buildings"). He described a world in which people live and travel about in mobile glass cubicles that can attach themselves to skyscraper-like frameworks, and in which all human knowledge can be disseminated to the world by radio and displayed automatically on giant book-like displays at streetcorners.

In his last years, Khlebnikov became fascinated by Slavic mythology and Pythagorean numerology, and drew up long "Tables of Destiny" decomposing historical intervals and dates into functions of the numbers 2 and 3.

Khlebnikov died of paralysis while a guest in the house of his friend Pyotr Miturich near Kresttsy.

A minor planet 3112 Velimir discovered by Soviet astronomer Nikolai Stepanovich Chernykh in 1977 is named after him.

External links

- The World of Velimir Khlebnikov [1] (English)
- Introduction to Khlebnikov [2] (English)
- Selected Poems by Khlebnikov [3] (Bilingual)
- Large Russian website devoted to life and works of Khlebnikov [4] (Russian)
- Velimir Khlebnikov: biography, poems [5] (Russian)
- Internet edition of Khlebnikov, *Tvoreniia*, Moscow, 1986 [6] (Russian)
- Poems. Khlebnikov [7] (Russian)
- Selected works [8] (Russian)
- Khlebnikov House-Museum in Astrakhan [9] (Russian)
- Studies of Khlebnikov's life and works [10] (Russian)
- "Artists of the World!" [11] in *Pusteblume* journal of translation (Bilingual)
- Digitized Russian avant-garde books [12]
- Listen to an interpretation of Khlebnikov's "Radio of the Future" at Acousmata music blog [13]
- English translations of 5 poems [14]
- English translations of 7 poems [15]

References

- Khlebnikov, Velimir, *The King of Time* (Schmidt, Paul, trans.; Douglas, Charlotte, ed.) Cambridge, Massachusetts: Harvard University Press, 1990. ISBN 0-674-50516-6
- MacKay, John. *Inscription and Modernity: From Wordsworth to Mandelstam.* Bloomington: Indiana University Press, 2006. ISBN 0-253-34749-1

Aleksei Kruchenykh

Aleksei Kruchenykh	
Kruchenykh, Moscow 1913	
Birth name	Aleksei Eliseevich Kruchenykh
Born	February 9, 1886 Olevka, Kherson province, Ukraine
Died	June 17, 1968 (aged 82) Moscow
Nationality	Russian
Field	Poetry, Collage, Artist's book
Movement	Russian Futurism Zaum
Works	*Universal War*, 1916

Aleksei Eliseevich Kruchenykh or **Kruchonykh** or **Kruchyonykh** (Russian: Алексе́й Елисе́евич Кручёных) (February 21, 1886 - June 17, 1968), a well-known poet of the Russian "Silver Age", was perhaps the most radical poet of Russian Futurism, a movement that included Vladimir Mayakovsky, David Burliuk and others. Together with Velimir Khlebnikov, Kruchenykh is considered the inventor of *zaum*. Kruchenykh wrote the libretto for the Futurist opera *Victory Over the Sun*, with sets provided by Kazimir Malevich. He married Olga Rozanova, an avant-garde artist, in 1912.

Most famous poem of Kruchenykh

Zaum	**Transliteration**
Дыр бул	Dyr bul shchyl
щыл	ubeshchur
убещур	skum
скум	vy so bu
вы со бу	r l ez
р л эз	

(1913)

External links

- On Kruchenykh [1] (English)
- Kruchenykh in Tiflis (from Chapter Nine of G. Janecek, *Zaum: The Transrational Poetry of Russian Futurism)* [2] (English)
- Biography and poems [3] (Russian)
- Biography, bibliography [4] (Russian)
- Four zaum poems [5] (Russian)
- Visual Poems 1917 - 1921 [6]
- Digitized Russian avant-garde books [12]
- English translations of 4 poems [7]

Article Sources and Contributors

Futurism *Source*: http://en.wikipedia.org/?oldid=390303315 *Contributors*: GeeJo

Divisionism *Source*: http://en.wikipedia.org/?oldid=372283742 *Contributors*:

Giovanni Segantini *Source*: http://en.wikipedia.org/?oldid=386728936 *Contributors*:

The Funeral of the Anarchist Galli *Source*: http://en.wikipedia.org/?oldid=390304276 *Contributors*: Ser Amantio di Nicolao

The City Rises (Boccioni) *Source*: http://en.wikipedia.org/?oldid=390304731 *Contributors*: Ser Amantio di Nicolao

Unique Forms of Continuity in Space *Source*: http://en.wikipedia.org/?oldid=384096461 *Contributors*:

Giacomo Balla *Source*: http://en.wikipedia.org/?oldid=390123454 *Contributors*:

Umberto Boccioni *Source*: http://en.wikipedia.org/?oldid=390304899 *Contributors*: GeeJo

Anton Giulio Bragaglia *Source*: http://en.wikipedia.org/?oldid=389058445 *Contributors*: 1 anonymous edits

David Burliuk *Source*: http://en.wikipedia.org/?oldid=387411817 *Contributors*: 1 anonymous edits

Wladimir Burliuk *Source*: http://en.wikipedia.org/?oldid=373243910 *Contributors*: Rjwilmsi

Mario Carli *Source*: http://en.wikipedia.org/?oldid=367956571 *Contributors*: DagosNavy

Carlo Carrà *Source*: http://en.wikipedia.org/?oldid=390304463 *Contributors*: Ser Amantio di Nicolao

Ambrogio Casati *Source*: http://en.wikipedia.org/?oldid=332042225 *Contributors*:

Primo Conti *Source*: http://en.wikipedia.org/?oldid=388436206 *Contributors*:

Tullio Crali *Source*: http://en.wikipedia.org/?oldid=389143284 *Contributors*:

Luigi De Giudici *Source*: http://en.wikipedia.org/?oldid=386768468 *Contributors*:

Fortunato Depero *Source*: http://en.wikipedia.org/?oldid=368356127 *Contributors*: Attilios

Nikolay Diulgheroff *Source*: http://en.wikipedia.org/?oldid=388498441 *Contributors*:

Gerardo Dottori *Source*: http://en.wikipedia.org/?oldid=343110900 *Contributors*: Grafen

Fillià *Source*: http://en.wikipedia.org/?oldid=330415578 *Contributors*:

Filippo Tommaso Marinetti *Source*: http://en.wikipedia.org/?oldid=390492391 *Contributors*:

Angiolo Mazzoni *Source*: http://en.wikipedia.org/?oldid=358558641 *Contributors*:

Aldo Palazzeschi *Source*: http://en.wikipedia.org/?oldid=389611359 *Contributors*: Ser Amantio di Nicolao

Giovanni Papini *Source*: http://en.wikipedia.org/?oldid=383822894 *Contributors*:

Luigi Russolo *Source*: http://en.wikipedia.org/?oldid=384705272 *Contributors*:

Valentine de Saint-Point *Source*: http://en.wikipedia.org/?oldid=313158814 *Contributors*:

Antonio Sant'Elia *Source*: http://en.wikipedia.org/?oldid=388019026 *Contributors*: Drmies

Jules Schmalzigaug *Source*: http://en.wikipedia.org/?oldid=380746655 *Contributors*: Epbr123

Gino Severini *Source*: http://en.wikipedia.org/?oldid=389339027 *Contributors*: Colonies Chris

Mario Sironi *Source*: http://en.wikipedia.org/?oldid=333472697 *Contributors*:

Ardengo Soffici *Source*: http://en.wikipedia.org/?oldid=359478076 *Contributors*: Superp

Vladimir Mayakovsky *Source*: http://en.wikipedia.org/?oldid=385250762 *Contributors*: 1 anonymous edits

Mikhail Larionov *Source*: http://en.wikipedia.org/?oldid=386158450 *Contributors*:

Natalia Goncharova *Source*: http://en.wikipedia.org/?oldid=386729186 *Contributors*:

Kazimir Malevich *Source*: http://en.wikipedia.org/?oldid=390384822 *Contributors*: Leningradartist

Velimir Khlebnikov *Source*: http://en.wikipedia.org/?oldid=382260130 *Contributors*:

Aleksei Kruchenykh *Source*: http://en.wikipedia.org/?oldid=386726782 *Contributors*:

Image Sources, Licenses and Contributors

File:Umberto Boccioni 001.jpg *Source*: http://bibliocm.bibliolabs.com/mwAnon/index.php?title=File:Umberto_Boccioni_001.jpg *License*: Public Domain *Contributors*: EDUCA33E, Emijrp, Prosfilaes

File:'Unique Forms of Continuity in Space', 1913 bronze by Umberto Boccioni.jpg *Source*: http://bibliocm.bibliolabs.com/mwAnon/index.php?title=File:'Unique_Forms_of_Continuity_in_Space',_1913_bronze_by_Umberto_Boccioni.jpg *License*: Public Domain *Contributors*: User:Wmpearl

File:Santelia01.jpg *Source*: http://bibliocm.bibliolabs.com/mwAnon/index.php?title=File:Santelia01.jpg *License*: unknown *Contributors*: AndreasPraefcke, Pullus In Fabula, Ronaldino, Shaqspeare, Str4nd, 3 anonymous edits

File:Blast2.jpg *Source*: http://bibliocm.bibliolabs.com/mwAnon/index.php?title=File:Blast2.jpg *License*: Public Domain *Contributors*: Elcobbola, Lukius, Man vyi, Sparkit, Truthkeeper88, Tyrenius, 2 anonymous edits

Image:Color star-en.svg *Source*: http://bibliocm.bibliolabs.com/mwAnon/index.php?title=File:Color_star-en.svg *License*: unknown *Contributors*: -

Image:Signac.jpg *Source*: http://bibliocm.bibliolabs.com/mwAnon/index.php?title=File:Signac.jpg *License*: unknown *Contributors*: AndreasPraefcke, Anna reg, Fransvannes, Infrogmation, Mu, Túrelio, Umherirrender, Wst, 2 anonymous edits

Image:Self_portrait_with_Felt_Hat.jpg *Source*: http://bibliocm.bibliolabs.com/mwAnon/index.php?title=File:Self_portrait_with_Felt_Hat.jpg *License*: Public Domain *Contributors*: Frank C. Müller, Macy, Vincent Steenberg, W., Zolo, 1 anonymous edits

Image:Giovanni Segantini 003.jpg *Source*: http://bibliocm.bibliolabs.com/mwAnon/index.php?title=File:Giovanni_Segantini_003.jpg *License*: Public Domain *Contributors*: AndreasPraefcke, Docu, Xenophon, 1 anonymous edits

Image:Giovanni Segantini 001.jpg *Source*: http://bibliocm.bibliolabs.com/mwAnon/index.php?title=File:Giovanni_Segantini_001.jpg *License*: Public Domain *Contributors*: AndreasPraefcke, Docu, 1 anonymous edits

Image:Giovanni Segantini 002.jpg *Source*: http://bibliocm.bibliolabs.com/mwAnon/index.php?title=File:Giovanni_Segantini_002.jpg *License*: unknown *Contributors*: -

File:PD-icon.svg *Source*: http://bibliocm.bibliolabs.com/mwAnon/index.php?title=File:PD-icon.svg *License*: Public Domain *Contributors*: User:Duesentrieb, User:Rfl

Image:Immagine-Umberto boccioni la città che sale.jpg *Source*: http://bibliocm.bibliolabs.com/mwAnon/index.php?title=File:Immagine-Umberto_boccioni_la_città_che_sale.jpg *License*: Public Domain *Contributors*: Mac'ero, Sergiodf

Image:'Unique Forms of Continuity in Space', 1913 bronze by Umberto Boccioni.jpg *Source*: http://bibliocm.bibliolabs.com/mwAnon/index.php?title=File:'Unique_Forms_of_Continuity_in_Space',_1913_bronze_by_Umberto_Boccioni.jpg *License*: Public Domain *Contributors*: User:Wmpearl

Image:Umberto-Boccioni.jpg *Source*: http://bibliocm.bibliolabs.com/mwAnon/index.php?title=File:Umberto-Boccioni.jpg *License*: unknown *Contributors*: -

Image:'States of Mind III; Those Who Stay', oil on canvas painting by Umberto Boccioni, 1911.jpg *Source*: http://bibliocm.bibliolabs.com/mwAnon/index.php?title=File:'States_of_Mind_III;_Those_Who_Stay',_oil_on_canvas_painting_by_Umberto_Boccioni,_1911.jpg *License*: unknown *Contributors*: Deadstar, Flominator, Wmpearl

Image:Ritratto di Busoni, 1916 (Roberto Biccioni).jpg *Source*: http://bibliocm.bibliolabs.com/mwAnon/index.php?title=File:Ritratto_di_Busoni,_1916_(Roberto_Biccioni).jpg *License*: unknown *Contributors*: Robert.Allen

Image:Umberto Boccioni - A strada entra nella casa.jpg *Source*: http://bibliocm.bibliolabs.com/mwAnon/index.php?title=File:Umberto_Boccioni_-_A_strada_entra_nella_casa.jpg *License*: unknown *Contributors*: GeeJo, Telrúnya, 1 anonymous edits

Image:Umberto Boccioni - Self-portrait, oil on canvas, 1905, Metropolitan Museum of Art.jpg *Source*: http://bibliocm.bibliolabs.com/mwAnon/index.php?title=File:Umberto_Boccioni_-_Self-portrait,_oil_on_canvas,_1905,_Metropolitan_Museum_of_Art.jpg *License*: unknown *Contributors*: Dcoetzee, Docu, Frank C. Müller, Ham, Sv1xv, Vincent Steenberg, Wmpearl

Image:Umberto Boccioni - Visioni simultanee.jpg *Source*: http://bibliocm.bibliolabs.com/mwAnon/index.php?title=File:Umberto_Boccioni_-_Visioni_simultanee.jpg *License*: unknown *Contributors*: Atamari, Telrúnya

Image:Vladimir Burliuk Khlebnikov.jpg *Source*: http://bibliocm.bibliolabs.com/mwAnon/index.php?title=File:Vladimir_Burliuk_Khlebnikov.jpg *License*: unknown *Contributors*: -

Image:uomo_con_pipa.jpg *Source*: http://bibliocm.bibliolabs.com/mwAnon/index.php?title=File:Uomo_con_pipa.jpg *License*: unknown *Contributors*: Luigi de Giudici

Image:Il_mio_studio_a_Tolmezzo.jpg *Source*: http://bibliocm.bibliolabs.com/mwAnon/index.php?title=File:Il_mio_studio_a_Tolmezzo.jpg *License*: Creative Commons Attribution 3.0 *Contributors*: Luigi de Giudici

Image:La_bella_sconosciuta.jpg *Source*: http://bibliocm.bibliolabs.com/mwAnon/index.php?title=File:La_bella_sconosciuta.jpg *License*: Creative Commons Attribution-Sharealike 3.0 *Contributors*: Luigi de Giudici

Image:Viaggiare.jpg *Source*: http://bibliocm.bibliolabs.com/mwAnon/index.php?title=File:Viaggiare.jpg *License*: Creative Commons Attribution-Sharealike 3.0 *Contributors*: Luigi de Giudici

Image:La_giostra.jpg *Source*: http://bibliocm.bibliolabs.com/mwAnon/index.php?title=File:La_giostra.jpg *License*: Creative Commons Attribution-Sharealike 3.0 *Contributors*: Luigi de Giudici

File:Fortunato Depero 1922.jpg *Source*: http://bibliocm.bibliolabs.com/mwAnon/index.php?title=File:Fortunato_Depero_1922.jpg *License*: unknown *Contributors*: -

File:Campari Soda.jpg *Source*: http://bibliocm.bibliolabs.com/mwAnon/index.php?title=File:Campari_Soda.jpg *License*: unknown *Contributors*: -

file:FilippoTommasoMarinetti.jpg *Source*: http://bibliocm.bibliolabs.com/mwAnon/index.php?title=File:FilippoTommasoMarinetti.jpg *License*: unknown *Contributors*: -

Image:Trento station columns.JPG *Source*: http://bibliocm.bibliolabs.com/mwAnon/index.php?title=File:Trento_station_columns.JPG *License*: Creative Commons Attribution-Sharealike 2.5 *Contributors*: Original uploader was Giac at en.wikipedia

Image:La Spezia - Palazzo delle Poste.jpg *Source*: http://bibliocm.bibliolabs.com/mwAnon/index.php?title=File:La_Spezia_-_Palazzo_delle_Poste.jpg *License*: Public Domain *Contributors*: Icarus83, 1 anonymous edits

file:Nunes Vais, Mario (1856-1932), Aldo Palazzeschi.jpg *Source*: http://bibliocm.bibliolabs.com/mwAnon/index.php?title=File:Nunes_Vais,_Mario_(1856-1932),_Aldo_Palazzeschi.jpg *License*: Public Domain *Contributors*: Mario

Nunes Vais (1856-1932).

Image:Luigi Russolo ca. 1916.gif *Source*: http://bibliocm.bibliolabs.com/mwAnon/index.php?title=File:Luigi_Russolo_ca._1916.gif *License*: Public Domain *Contributors*: Lukius, Mu, Sparkit

Image:Santelia03.jpg *Source*: http://bibliocm.bibliolabs.com/mwAnon/index.php?title=File:Santelia03.jpg *License*: unknown *Contributors*: Antonio Sant'Elia

Image:Santelia02.jpg *Source*: http://bibliocm.bibliolabs.com/mwAnon/index.php?title=File:Santelia02.jpg *License*: unknown *Contributors*: Antonio Sant'Elia

Image:Santelia01.jpg *Source*: http://bibliocm.bibliolabs.com/mwAnon/index.php?title=File:Santelia01.jpg *License*: unknown *Contributors*: AndreasPraefcke, Pullus In Fabula, Ronaldino, Shaqspeare, Str4nd, 3 anonymous edits

Image:Schmalzigaug - Impression in a Dance Hall.JPG *Source*: http://bibliocm.bibliolabs.com/mwAnon/index.php?title=File:Schmalzigaug_-_Impression_in_a_Dance_Hall.JPG *License*: Public Domain *Contributors*: painting of Jules Schmalzigaug, own photo

Image:Schmalzigaug - Light.JPG *Source*: http://bibliocm.bibliolabs.com/mwAnon/index.php?title=File:Schmalzigaug_-_Light.JPG *License*: unknown *Contributors*: -

Image:Terras Schmalzigaug.jpg *Source*: http://bibliocm.bibliolabs.com/mwAnon/index.php?title=File:Terras_Schmalzigaug.jpg *License*: unknown *Contributors*: -

File:Gino_Severini.jpg *Source*: http://bibliocm.bibliolabs.com/mwAnon/index.php?title=File:Gino_Severini.jpg *License*: anonymous-EU *Contributors*: Bohème, Marshall46, Rcbutcher, Vincent Steenberg

file:Mayakovsky 1929 a.jpg *Source*: http://bibliocm.bibliolabs.com/mwAnon/index.php?title=File:Mayakovsky_1929_a.jpg *License*: Public Domain *Contributors*: Butko, Martin H., Valdemus, 1 anonymous edits

Image:Mayakovsky-kak-delat-stixi.png *Source*: http://bibliocm.bibliolabs.com/mwAnon/index.php?title=File:Mayakovsky-kak-delat-stixi.png *License*: unknown *Contributors*: -

Image:Vladimir mayakovsky and lilya brik.jpg *Source*: http://bibliocm.bibliolabs.com/mwAnon/index.php?title=File:Vladimir_mayakovsky_and_lilya_brik.jpg *License*: unknown *Contributors*: Original uploader was Humus sapiens at en.wikipedia

Image:Plakat mayakowski gross.jpg *Source*: http://bibliocm.bibliolabs.com/mwAnon/index.php?title=File:Plakat_mayakowski_gross.jpg *License*: unknown *Contributors*: Vladimir Mayakovsky (1893-1930)

File:Monumento di Vladimir Majakovskij a Novkuzneck.jpg *Source*: http://bibliocm.bibliolabs.com/mwAnon/index.php?title=File:Monumento_di_Vladimir_Majakovskij_a_Novkuzneck.jpg *License*: unknown *Contributors*: Alesseus Original uploader was Alesseus at it.wikipedia

File:Goncharova self portret yellow lilies.jpg *Source*: http://bibliocm.bibliolabs.com/mwAnon/index.php?title=File:Goncharova_self_portret_yellow_lilies.jpg *License*: unknown *Contributors*: -

File:Self-Portrait (1908 or 1910-1911).jpg *Source*: http://bibliocm.bibliolabs.com/mwAnon/index.php?title=File:Self-Portrait_(1908_or_1910-1911).jpg *License*: unknown *Contributors*: Edgar Allan Poe, Szczebrzeszynski, Vincent Steenberg

File:Malevich.black-square.jpg *Source*: http://bibliocm.bibliolabs.com/mwAnon/index.php?title=File:Malevich.black-square.jpg *License*: unknown *Contributors*: Bastique, Emijrp, Kaganer, Rtc, Shakko, Svencb, Thuresson, Vincent Steenberg, Wizardist

File:Malevich-selfportrait-small.jpg *Source*: http://bibliocm.bibliolabs.com/mwAnon/index.php?title=File:Malevich-selfportrait-small.jpg *License*: unknown *Contributors*: Английская Википедия

File:Flowergirl.jpg *Source*: http://bibliocm.bibliolabs.com/mwAnon/index.php?title=File:Flowergirl.jpg *License*: unknown *Contributors*: Edgar Allan Poe, Shakko

File:Bathers.jpg *Source*: http://bibliocm.bibliolabs.com/mwAnon/index.php?title=File:Bathers.jpg *License*: unknown *Contributors*: Edgar Allan Poe, Shakko

File:Malewitsch4.jpg *Source*: http://bibliocm.bibliolabs.com/mwAnon/index.php?title=File:Malewitsch4.jpg *License*: unknown *Contributors*: Überraschungsbilder, 2 anonymous edits

File:Taking in the Rye Kazimir Malevich 1911.jpeg *Source*: http://bibliocm.bibliolabs.com/mwAnon/index.php?title=File:Taking_in_the_Rye_Kazimir_Malevich_1911.jpeg *License*: unknown *Contributors*: MarmadukePercy

File:The Knifegrinder Kazimir Malevich.jpeg *Source*: http://bibliocm.bibliolabs.com/mwAnon/index.php?title=File:The_Knifegrinder_Kazimir_Malevich.jpeg *License*: unknown *Contributors*: MarmadukePercy

File:Head of a Peasant Girl.jpg *Source*: http://bibliocm.bibliolabs.com/mwAnon/index.php?title=File:Head_of_a_Peasant_Girl.jpg *License*: unknown *Contributors*: -

File:Bureau and Room.jpg *Source*: http://bibliocm.bibliolabs.com/mwAnon/index.php?title=File:Bureau_and_Room.jpg *License*: unknown *Contributors*: Edgar Allan Poe, Ilse@, Sasha Krotov

File:Portrait of Matiushin Kazimir Malevich 1913.jpeg *Source*: http://bibliocm.bibliolabs.com/mwAnon/index.php?title=File:Portrait_of_Matiushin_Kazimir_Malevich_1913.jpeg *License*: unknown *Contributors*: MarmadukePercy

File:Cow and Fiddle.jpg *Source*: http://bibliocm.bibliolabs.com/mwAnon/index.php?title=File:Cow_and_Fiddle.jpg *License*: unknown *Contributors*: Edgar Allan Poe, Santosga, Shakko

File:Englishman in Moscow.jpg *Source*: http://bibliocm.bibliolabs.com/mwAnon/index.php?title=File:Englishman_in_Moscow.jpg *License*: unknown *Contributors*: Edgar Allan Poe, Ilse@, Mattes, Serge Lachinov

File:Composition with the Mona Lisa Kazimir Malevich 1914.jpeg *Source*: http://bibliocm.bibliolabs.com/mwAnon/index.php?title=File:Composition_with_the_Mona_Lisa_Kazimir_Malevich_1914.jpeg *License*: unknown *Contributors*: MarmadukePercy

File:Black circle.jpg *Source*: http://bibliocm.bibliolabs.com/mwAnon/index.php?title=File:Black_circle.jpg *License*: unknown *Contributors*: EugeneZelenko, FrancisTyers, Man vyi, Nk, Nyttend, Shakko, Svencb, Talmoryair, Vincent Steenberg, Yelzin, 1 anonymous edits

File:Malevich-Suprematism..jpg *Source*: http://bibliocm.bibliolabs.com/mwAnon/index.php?title=File:Malevich-Suprematism..jpg *License*: unknown *Contributors*: Edgar Allan Poe, Ilse@, Vincent Steenberg

File:Malevici06.jpg *Source*: http://bibliocm.bibliolabs.com/mwAnon/index.php?title=File:Malevici06.jpg *License*: GNU Free Documentation License *Contributors*: Alex Bakharev, Maksim, Nk, Talmoryair, 1 anonymous edits

File:Malevitj.jpg *Source*: http://bibliocm.bibliolabs.com/mwAnon/index.php?title=File:Malevitj.jpg *License*: unknown *Contributors*: Albedo-ukr, AndreasPraefcke, Butko, Thuresson

File:Malevich - Boy.jpg *Source*: http://bibliocm.bibliolabs.com/mwAnon/index.php?title=File:Malevich_-_Boy.jpg *License*: unknown *Contributors*: Edgar Allan Poe, Jmabel

File:Malevich cavalry.jpg *Source*: http://bibliocm.bibliolabs.com/mwAnon/index.php?title=File:Malevich_cavalry.jpg *License*: unknown *Contributors*: Alex Bakharev, Григорий А. Харьков, 1 anonymous edits

File:Malevich Summer Landscape.JPG *Source*: http://bibliocm.bibliolabs.com/mwAnon/index.php?title=File:Malevich_Summer_Landscape.JPG *License*: Public Domain *Contributors*: Alex Bakharev, Shakko

File:Malevich142.jpg *Source*: http://bibliocm.bibliolabs.com/mwAnon/index.php?title=File:Malevich142.jpg *License*: unknown *Contributors*: Albedo-ukr, Alex Bakharev, Montalcino, Svencb

file:Chlebnikow.jpg *Source*: http://bibliocm.bibliolabs.com/mwAnon/index.php?title=File:Chlebnikow.jpg *License*: Public Domain *Contributors*: A.Savin, Henry Merrivale, Meladina, Szczebrzeszynski, Szwedzki

The cover image herein is used under a Creative Commons License and may be reused or reproduced under that same license.

http://upload.wikimedia.org/wikipedia/commons/b/b8/Umberto_Boccioni_002.jpg

CPSIA information can be obtained at www.ICGtesting.com
Printed in the USA
BVOW080539080312

284675BV00003B/26/P

9 781170 680964